Cooperative Enterprise

Cooperative Enterprise

Facing the Challenge of Globalization

Stefano Zamagni

Professor of Economics, University of Bologna and Johns Hopkins University, Bologna Center, Italy

Vera Zamagni

Professor of Economic History, University of Bologna and Johns Hopkins University, Bologna Center, Italy

Edward Elgar
Cheltenham, UK • Northampton, MA, USA

Originally published in Italian by Il Mulino as *La Cooperazione*.

Published by
Edward Elgar Publishing Limited
The Lypiatts
15 Lansdown Road
Cheltenham
Glos GL50 2JA
UK

Edward Elgar Publishing, Inc.
William Pratt House
9 Dewey Court
Northampton
Massachusetts 01060
USA

A catalogue record for this book is available from the British Library

Library of Congress Control Number: 2009941253

Mixed Sources
Product group from well-managed
forests and other controlled sources
www.fsc.org Cert no. SA-COC-1565
© 1996 Forest Stewardship Council

ISBN 978 1 84844 974 9 (cased)

Typeset by Cambrian Typesetters, Camberley, Surrey
Printed and bound by MPG Books Group, UK

Contents

Preface

Co-operation touches no man's fortune; seeks no plunder; causes no distur-
bance in society; gives no trouble to statesmen; it enters into no secret associations; it needs no trades union to protect its interests; it contemplates no
violence; it subverts no order; it envys no dignity; it accepts no gift, nor asks
any favour; it keeps no terms with the idle, and it will break no faith with the
industrious. It is neither mendicant, servile, nor offensive; ... it means self-
help, self-dependence, and such share of the common competence as labour
shall earn or thought can win (George Jacob Holyoake, *The History of
Cooperation*, 1906)

Why a book on cooperative enterprises today? What is the sense in being
concerned with cooperation at the dawn of the twenty-first century?
These are not idle questions, and the answers cannot be taken for
granted, considering the large number of people who think that as a form
of enterprise the cooperative has now been superseded, a fine and noble
memory, an economic mode that certainly exalted solidarity but that has
now become an awkward anachronism. It is the purpose of this book to
show that those who think in these terms are mistaken. Jon Elster (1989,
p. 99) expresses the sceptics' viewpoint perfectly in asking 'If cooperative ownership is so desirable, then why are there so few cooperatives?'
We shall try to explain that the sceptical attitude is unfounded, because
it stems from an erroneous way of conceiving the nexus between market
economy and capitalistic economy.

Cooperation is a quintessentially morphogenetic phenomenon characterized by a high degree of change, evolving both for internal causes
and in response to economic change in the surrounding society. In the
nineteenth and much of the twentieth centuries producer, labour,
consumer and user cooperatives were formed and grew in the economically advanced countries in order to enable the poorer segments of the
population to increase their market power and so to ward off social
exclusion. But in the course of the last quarter-century, more or less in
conjunction with the transition from industrial to post-industrial society,
cooperation has discovered new purposes, new reasons for being. Some
are strictly economic (in selected segments of the economy, such as

personal services, cooperatives have displayed a specific advantage in efficiency over the capitalistic form of enterprise). Others concern the consolidation of the liberal social order (by helping to reduce inequalities in income distribution and to expand the space for democracy, the cooperative movement is a powerful creator of social capital, that is, networks of trust among citizens). In addition, the cooperative is a form of enterprise well suited to sustaining economic growth in the emerging economies and in the sectors and regions least open to international investment. This book will set out these reasons, describing the concrete, practical effects with reference to contemporary societies.

Finding the new *raison d'être* for cooperatives in the era of globalization does not imply that the cooperative movement by this alone is capable of taking up and successfully meeting the challenges it faces. One difficulty in particular overshadows all: how to avoid the risk that the unavoidable need for capital to finance growth may lead the cooperative to water down its identity and finally lose sight of the fact that the distinctive property of this form of enterprise is to always keep together co-substantial, mutual solidarity and economic activity. The danger of this mortal trap will be broadly discussed in the course of this book.

Let us offer our sincere thanks to the many friends and colleagues with whom we have had a chance to discuss – and sometimes to argue over – these themes. Aware that we are inevitably leaving out many, we thank in particular: Antonio Argandoña, Patrizia Battilani, Giacomo Becattini, Leonardo Becchetti, Avner Ben-Ner, Giuseppe Bonfante, Carlo Borzaga, Luk Bourkaert, Luigino Bruni, Pietro Cafaro, Partha Das Gupta, Gregory Dow, Adriano Di Pietro, Giulio Ecchia, Dann Finn, Enrico Giovannetti, Bruno Jossa, Andrea Leonardi, Massimiliano Marzo, Antonio Matacena, Mario Mazzoleni, Jan McPherson, Vittorio Pelligra, Pierluigi Sacco, Lorenzo Sacconi, Mario Salani, Amartya Sen and Laszlo Zsolnai. We should also thank our students in the University of Bologna's Master's Programme in the Economics of Cooperation, the first in Italy, instituted in 1996, after years of efforts to bring cooperation finally into the official catalogue.

We dedicate this book to our marvellous grandchildren Alice, Matteo, Federico and Margherita, who are already coming to see that the course of life is traced out walking together.

1. Introduction

1.1 COOPERATION AND THE CIVIL MARKET

The cooperative is a genuine, two-faced Janus. It combines two distinct if not conflicting dimensions: the economic dimension of an enterprise that operates within the market and accepts its logic; and the social dimension of an institution that pursues meta-economic aims and produces positive externalities for other agents and for the entire community. This dual nature is what makes the cooperative so difficult to explain and so hard to govern. If conventional economics has trouble explaining the conduct of an agent who does not pursue only self-interested ends, social science also has trouble understanding how an agent like the cooperative can successfully act through the market to forge strong ties of solidarity and advanced forms of participatory democracy.

What makes the governance of a cooperative enterprise arduous is the dual nature of the symbolic codes – market code, social code – that shape its identity. As more than a century of history demonstrates so well, there have been times or phases in which the market code has dominated, making it impossible to distinguish cooperatives from other corporations; and others in which the social code has enjoyed an excessive preponderance, leading to economic decline or marginal status. In both these cases, whenever one of these aspects is sacrificed to the other, the cooperative is denatured, losing its identity. Maintaining a dynamic equilibrium between the two codes and ensuring that the result of their mutual contamination is strategic complementarity is the great challenge for the cooperative movement in the twenty-first century.

Later on we shall discuss how that challenge can be met. Right away, though, we can see why cooperatives have been likened to bumblebees. According to the laws of Newtonian physics, apparently, the bumblebee cannot fly – its wingspan is insufficient to support its body weight. Yet bumblebees do, in fact, fly. In the same way, for conventional economic theory the cooperative cannot function in the long run, because its non-economic purposes are seen as a stumbling block to the attainment of the economic ones. So if cooperatives do in fact survive over time, it is held, this is because exogenous, compensating factors are brought into play: tax allowances, favourable legislation, political support. That this is not the case is perfectly well known, even though in some historical settings those factors have played important roles, and notably so in Italy. So we must go beyond technicalities to the core of a form of enterprise such as the cooperative one that has originated and spread in nearly all the countries of Europe, and also in the USA and Canada as well as in Asia and Africa, in the presence of radically different legislations and tax provisions.

If Einstein's physics had to arise before the flight of the bumblebee could be explained, it will be necessary for economics to admit – with the proper dose of humility – that the rationality of individuals pursuing their own personal self-interest is not necessarily the sole economic rationality; and therefore that the economic action of enterprises like cooperatives, driven by a different set of motivations, also represents a form of rationality, albeit different from the merely instrumental rationality of the capitalist enterprise. Embarking upon this line of thought means acknowledging that the market economy is a genus and the capitalist economy, however important it may be today, but one species within it. Similarly, it means positing that in order to work properly a free market economy does not necessarily postulate Darwinian survival of the fittest, a market characterized by what the American economist Sherwin Rosen has called the 'superstar effect': winner take all, loser leave all.

Instead we must be prepared to recognize that there also exist civil markets, those that tend to close economic and social gaps and enable everyone – individuals and groups – to be a part of the economic game, activating inclusive mechanisms (Bruni and Zamagni, 2007). In civil markets those least endowed with resources or least efficient are cared for not by redistributing the wealth produced by those better endowed, but during the production phase itself, by allowing the disadvantaged too to participate. This, it turns out, is the prime mission of the cooperative movement today: to extend the space occupied by civil markets and so protect the market economy itself from the risk of a slow but steady degeneration. Even the Italian liberal economist Luigi Einaudi took a sympathetic view of the cooperative movement precisely because of its ability to strengthen the free market system. In 1941 he declared his admiration for the utopian socialists as 'among the greatest creators and promoters of that grand cooperative movement, which has changed the face of some human societies'.

The practical example that best illustrates the civil market mode of cooperative enterprises' operation is what is known as 'cooperative promotion'. In Italy, for example, co-ops allocate 3 per cent of their net operating result each year to form or support, by creating mutual funds under the 1992 law,[1] other cooperative enterprises – which, when in operation, will be in competition with the former in the market. This is diametrically opposed to what happens in the Darwinian marketplace, where existing firms never seek to create or assist rivals. As Adam Smith (1723–90) had so clearly sensed, the more or less secret desire of any capitalist firm is to be the sole company in the market, so as to exert monopoly power. A close look at his works shows how concerned he was over the danger that successful firms would maintain their grasp on the society. In fact, just a few years after his *Wealth of Nations* in 1776, the founder of modern economics actually wrote to his publisher, fearing that the book would not sell because it was overly critical of the holders of economic power. Smith's concern was not vain; and indeed it was not until more than a century later that a number of countries, first and foremost the USA, began to pass antitrust laws for authoritative government intervention to protect the market from its own inherent tendencies.

But we can see that cooperatives practiced inter-firm solidarity from the very beginning. One of the principles of the Rochdale Society of Equitable Pioneers (founded in 1844) reads: 'Cooperation among co-operatives. Co-operatives serve their members most effectively and strengthen the co-operative movement by working together through local, national, regional and international structures.' To be sure, the forms of promotion have evolved over the years, even radically. At first real services prevailed (consulting, tutoring, training). Today financial services are more important. But the spirit is the same: if cooperation is good for the society and not just for the co-op's own members, then no cooperator must impede the market competition, the word itself deriving from the Latin '*cum petere*' or literally, tend together to a common goal. That goal is to enable the citizen-consumer to exercise some sort of

---

[1]   The four Italian cooperative umbrella organizations each have a fund: Legacoop's 'Coopfond', Confcooperative's 'Fondosviluppo', AGCI's 'Generalfondo' and UNCI's 'Promocoop'. Co-ops not belonging to any of these four umbrella organizations pay their 3 per cent to the Ministry for Productive Activities.

sovereignty over the market – that is, to choose freely between the alternatives offered by rival providers.

The creation of these mutual funds demonstrates that the cooperative movement has fully understood Marshall's metaphor of the tree and the woods: there can be no lasting growth of the tree – the single cooperative – save as part of the harmonious development of the forest of cooperation in general. And above all it has understood that there exists an alternative to the typically capitalistic process that Joseph Schumpeter called 'creative destruction' – in which the capitalistic market creates while destroying and destroys in order to create. 'The kind of competition that really matters,' wrote the great Austrian economist, 'is not price competition but the competition that destroys the old commodity to replace it with the new' (Schumpeter, 1934, p. 74). We are well aware of the many economic advantages generated by this mechanism. But we are equally familiar with its brutality, its harmful social and political repercussions. And it is clear that if creative destruction may enjoy some legitimacy as long as the value of what is created is greater than that of what is destroyed, that legitimacy ends when – as is the case today – the relation is inverted. We call the specific form of competition practiced by cooperatives 'competitive cooperation', which is a powerful antidote to the damage that would be done by 'positional competition' – the sort of competition sparked by the superstar effect – if it were to remain the sole form of competition admitted in the market (Zamagni et al., 2006).

1.2 MARKET ECONOMY AND CAPITALIST ECONOMY

These considerations imply a broader question: can the reasons of the cooperative movement be defended within the framework of a market economy? This is no idle question, because as we shall see there have been a good number of attempts – in France, in Britain and in the USA – to use the movement for anti-market purposes. Yet as we shall show, not only is cooperation not antithetical to the market, it actually postulates a market economy. Where, then, does the concern implied in our question originate? It stems from a serious conceptual confusion, the tendency to see as identical, as co-extensive, the market economy and the capitalist economy. This identity has been negated by history – the market economy arose centuries before capitalism – and it is theoretically unfounded. Capitalism constitutes a model of society, but the market is simply a way of organizing the economic sphere. Let us try to explain.

Between the end of the thirteenth century and the mid-sixteenth century there arose and flourished in Umbria and Tuscany a social order for which Italy was justly renowned, that of 'urban civilization'. What were its distinctive features? First, to use a term from our own era, there was what we could call 'participatory' democracy. With its ups and downs, this democratic system admittedly left openings for autocratic government, but at the same time it established the desirability of self-government and collective responsibility for territorial management. Its units may have been small, but they were real cities to all intents and purposes, with the typical structure of urban life: a central square (*agora*), the cathedral, the town halls, the merchants' and guilds' hall, the marketplace (where negotiations and trade were conducted), the homes of wealthy bourgeois families, the monasteries and the churches, which were not only the locus of religious ceremonies, but also the seats of the town's confraternities. It was in these places – not at all ideal-typical but practical and concrete – that these communities cultivated those 'civic virtues' that then as now define a truly civil society: trust, reciprocity, fraternity.

The economy of the Italian cities consisted of manufacturers and merchants, plus sailors in the coastal cities. To the merchants went the task of opening new markets, sometimes very distant markets (Marco Polo who reached China is an excellent example), for the sale of the products of manufacturing and the imports of everything that could be useful. The merchants were not only the most active agents for cultural exchanges but also the most active producers of organizational innovation for enterprises: the *commenda,* predecessor to the modern corporation; insurance; double-entry book-keeping, definitively systematized by the Franciscan monk Luca Pacioli in 1494; the chambers of merchants; letters of exchange; the *Monti di Pietà* (pawn banks), all institutions without which sustainable economic development throughout the territory could never have taken place (Bruni and Zamagni, 2007).

There arose, in these cities, two other dimensions to social life that are essential to understanding subsequent developments. The first was the continual reinvention of the present starting from the past. It was the humanists above all who vouchsafed this standpoint to the future of Western civilization. The texts and artefacts of ancient Greece and Rome were recovered, reconstructed philologically, interpreted and brought out again for new reasons, new purposes, in which elements of the past and a new cultural temperament blended harmoniously to produce new 'modes'. The second was the patronage of artistic durable goods. The patron was not just a philanthropist, donating part of their income or wealth with no interest in how it was used. Typically, if not always, the art patron was an entrepreneur, putting resources and business know-how at the service of a cause that was in the community interest. A perfect illustration is the wool merchant/manufacturers of Florence – to whom we owe the project design, construction and financing of the city's cathedral. This was what lay behind the Florentine flowering of decorated churches, ever larger, ever more monumental, which gave rise to the market in art products.

It was the new bourgeoisie that continued with the building of public palaces, fountains and splendid private mansions, thus increasing the demand for the services of architects, sculptors, painters, decorators, furniture craftsmen, gardeners and so on. Meanwhile, dress too became more and more elaborate, more precious, while ceramics and silverware (another of the age's inventions) also grew into minor art forms. Income began to be invested in durable art goods – finally diversifying away from the only forms of expenditure practised until then: servants, vict-uals and equipment for hunt and warfare. By this point, a solid tradition had been established, but a long time would have to pass before it could reveal all its potential.

In a word, the linchpin of the urban civilization is the market econ-omy, in its modern sense. Three pillars of the market economy can show us its specificity. The first is the division of labour, a way of organizing production that enables everyone, even the less physically or mentally gifted, to perform useful work. For without the division of labour only the more gifted would be able, unaided, to procure what they need. The second principle is the priority of growth, hence accumulation. Wealth needs to be invested productively, in this view, not only as a reserve against future contingencies, but also out of responsibility to the community and to future generations. A particularly eloquent definition of the concept of growth comes from Coluccio Salutati, who wrote, following his great predecessor Albertano da Brescia: 'To dedicate oneself honestly to an honest activity may be a holy thing, holier than living in idleness and solitude. Because holiness attained through the rustic life serves only oneself ... but the holiness of the industrious life raises up the lives of many' (cited in Nuccio, 1987). Clearly, here we are very far from the medieval canon condemning all economic production in excess of the strictly necessary (*'Est cupiditas plus habendi quam oportet'*) (To possess more than what is necessary is greed).

The third principle of the market economy, finally, is freedom of enterprise. Those endowed with creativity, a good propensity for risk and the ability to coordinate the work of many others (*ars combinatoria*) – the three essential qualities of the entrepreneur – must be left free to undertake initiatives without the need for prior authorization from a sovereign or bureaucracy, because the active and industrious life (*vita activa et negociosa*) is a value in itself, not just a means to other ends. Freedom of enterprise implies economic competition. The *cum petere* that takes place in the market is the direct consequence of freedom of enterprise, and at the same time reproduces that freedom. In a competitive economy the final outcome of the process does not depend on the will of some overarching body – as would be the case in planned economies, now practically vanished, where the prices of goods and services, their quantities, employment levels and so on, are decided politically – but on the 'free' interaction of persons, each 'rationally' pursuing their own 'objective' under a well-defined set of 'rules'. We must grasp the meaning of these four key words.

Saying that interaction must be 'free' means that no agent can be constrained by force or a state of necessity that deprives them of their freedom to decide. So a slave, a totally uninformed person, or a person in absolute indigence does not meet the requirements of freedom necessary to the correct deployment of the mechanism of competition. The qualification that one must pursue one's interest 'rationally' postulates economic agents' ability to calculate, that is, both to evaluate the costs and benefits of the options available and to adopt a criterion for choice. Note that despite what one so often reads, this criterion does not necessarily correspond to the maximization of profit (or utility). So it is not true that competition necessarily posits acceptance of the logic of profit. For the 'objective' of market participants may be self-interested or mutual; it may be directed to the well-being of a particular group or category of persons, or to the common good. What matters is that each person knows the objective they intend to pursue; otherwise the requirement of rationality is not met.

Finally, competition requires well-defined 'rules' known to all participants and enforced by an authority that is not party to the game. This authority may be the state or a supranational agency, or civil society itself, if properly equipped for the task. A concrete instance was the formulation of the celebrated *Lex mercatoria* and the Law of the Sea to reduce the socially perverse effects of unregulated competition. These laws were designed and introduced by merchants themselves (Greif, 2006), not by any sovereign. It was not until the seventeenth century after the Peace of Westphalia and the birth of the nation-state that these laws came into state jurisdiction. They had two fundamental provisions: a ban on the concentration of power in the hands of one or a few agents in the form of monopoly or oligopoly; and a ban on fraud or deceit in market transactions.

Through emulation, competition stimulates the spirit of enterprise and imposes rational calculation. Where there is competition, positions of rent and privilege cannot prevail. To be sure, competition is costly, but it improves quality by leading to greater customization of products, giving them an identity; as in politics, where democracy certainly entails high costs but keeps the quality of civic life from deteriorating. As Bernardino of Siena said so forcefully in his 'Vulgar Sermons' in 1427, if the end for which an enterprise is conducted is the common good, the social costs of competition will never be too high.

Then, as now, freedom, rationality and rules are three elements that identify a market economy, whatever kind it is. What can vary is the fourth element, namely the specific end pursued by the participants: either the common good or the total good. The common good is the object of the civil market economy; the total good that of the capitalistic market economy.

1.3   COMMON GOOD VERSUS TOTAL GOOD

Starting in the seventeenth century the civil market economy began its transformation into the capitalistic market economy, though the definitive triumph of capitalism as a social model did not come until the industrial revolution. Capitalism gradually replaced the logic of the common good with that of the total good, that is, the 'profit motive'. Productive activity was directed to a single purpose, the maximization of profits for distribution among the investors in proportion to their share of the capital. With the industrial revolution, the principle '*fiat productio et pereat homo*' (production at the expense of man) was finally established, sanctioning the radical separation between the suppliers of capital and the suppliers of labour and definitively abandoning the old principle of action to the measure of man ('*omnium rerum mensura homo*') (man is the yardstick of everything) that originally underlay the market economy. The simplest way to see that the profit motive as such was not a constituent element of the market economy is to refer to the writings of the fifteenth-century civil humanists (such as Leonardo Bruni, Matteo Palmieri, Antonino of Florence and Bernardino da Feltre) and the civil economists of the eighteenth century (Antonio Genovesi, Giacinto Dragonetti, Cesare Beccaria, Pietro Verri and Giandomenico Romagnosi). A constant theme in their work is that market activities need to be oriented to the common good, from which alone they derive their legitimacy, or rather their justification (Zamagni, 2008).

The question is: what exactly is the difference between 'common good' and 'total good'? A metaphor may serve. While the total good can be rendered by the concept of the sum, in which the addends represent the good of the individual persons (or groups), the common good is more like a product, in which the multipliers are the good of the individuals (or groups). The meaning of the metaphor is intuitive: even if some of the addends cancel one another out, the total may remain positive. Indeed, it could happen that if the objective is maximizing the total good, it may be best to cancel the good (or the welfare) of some persons, if the welfare gains of others more than offset the loss. In a multiplication this is not the case, because the reduction to zero of even one single factor makes the entire product nil.

In other words, the logic of the common good does not admit trade-offs. You cannot sacrifice the welfare of someone – whatever their life situation or social position – to better that of others, even if the gain is more than proportional to the loss, for the fundamental reason that that 'someone' always enjoys basic human rights. For the logic of total good, however, that someone is an individual agent, that is, a subject identified with a particular utility function, and utilities can be readily summed up (or compared), because they are faceless; they do not express an identity, a personal history. The principle of total good follows directly from the utilitarian philosophy of Jeremy Bentham (1789), by which the rational person choosing among two or more alternatives will choose the one that maximizes the sum of the individual utilities associated with the individual options. As the great liberal Austrian economist Joseph Schumpeter would write of utilitarianism (1954):

> This system of ideas, developed in the 18th century, recognizes no normative principle other than individual interest. The essential fact is this: that whether it be cause or effect, this philosophy expresses only too well the spirit of *social irresponsibility* that characterized the secular, or secularized, state of the 19th century. (p. 127, emphasis added)

A twofold conclusion follows. First, it is simply not true that the action of enterprise is inevitably characterized by the search for profit; hence it is not true that the sole admissible form of enterprise is the capitalist firm. An entrepreneur is a person who, with the endowment mentioned, can produce value added, regardless of their motivation. The second conclusion is a reassurance to supporters of the market economy – ourselves included – that a future expansion of cooperative enterprise would in no way mean the disappearance or even the weakening of the market as an institution. Quite the contrary: it would significantly strengthen the market, in line with the urgings of many analysts concerned with the negative performance of the capitalistic market. Rajan and Zingales (2003), for example, write:

> We believe that capitalism – today more precisely described as the free enterprise system – is, in its ideal form, the best system for allocating resources and incentives. But the form that capitalism assumes in the majority of nations is far distant from that ideal. Many of the accusations made against capitalism … refer to existing corrupt and non-competitive systems, more than to the authentic free enterprise system. (p. 324)

And the authors continue:

> The worst enemies of capitalism are not union agitators with their corrosive critique of the system, but the managers in pinstriped suits who sing the praises of competitive markets in every speech while they try to suppress them with every action. (p. 325)

It is because they continue to maintain that the capitalistic is the only possible form of market that so many academics, and no few policy makers, are so alarmed at the growth and spread of cooperatives and of social and civil enterprises generally. Certainly capitalism posits and guarantees free markets, but the converse does not hold. One can no doubt erect an economy based on the free market without adopting the principle of the total good but instead that of the common good. Henry Hansmann has written (1996) that

> Freedom of enterprise is an essential characteristic of the most advanced market economies. Capitalism, by contrast, is contingent. It is simply that particular form of ownership of *patrons* that most often, but not always, proves to be efficient based on available technology. (p. 292, emphasis in original).

This is tantamount to classifying the market economy as a genus, of which capitalism is only one species. To generalize somewhat, we can say that the market economy is justified first of all by the principle of liberty, a liberty of which the capitalist economy is but one of various possible forms.

2. The birth of cooperative enterprise: where, when, how

2.1 WHERE COOPERATIVES AROSE

The birth of cooperative enterprise coincided with the advent of the industrial revolution, but the sense of solidarity and concern for the poor antedated it by centuries. Medieval cities, beginning in Italy, developed an inclusive institutional structure in which the representatives of the productive strata (merchants and craftsmen) formed both organizations that administered their interests in a cooperative fashion (guilds and merchants' chambers) and organizations that looked after those who for one reason or another were not part of the productive classes or who were in temporary distress: hospitals, orphanages, convent schools, pawn banks, dowry funds, public lending institutions, poor laws. All this was coordinated within a network of market relations that harmonized social life within the city, not excluding any of its members a priori, and carried out trade externally, thus increasing the overall prosperity.

The productive enterprise in its modern version was then in its infancy; its typical form was the family run craftsman's shop. Only the great merchant companies, with their large size and, very early on, their organization by equity shares, foreshadowed the characteristics that firms would take on later. With the industrial revolution in the eighteenth century, the 'capitalist' form of enterprise, the public limited company, became solidly established. The holders of equity capital entered into contracts with all the other factors of production, paying them the minimum possible for their services and distributing the entire gain as remuneration of the capital advanced.

At this point the forms of social solidarity needed to adapt. The purpose was no longer just to prevent the ruin of the less productive or non-self-sufficient social groups; rather, solidarity had to counter the all-powerful role of capital at the expense of labour, which was no longer independent and self-coordinated as in the medieval craft guilds but regimented in huge factories, dominated by rigid hierarchy and directed to the best possible use of machinery and the greatest possible division of labour. Thus alongside charitable institutions for the poor, which continued to exist, there arose trade unions to protect workers' interest within the factory. At the same time the idea began to gain ground that citizens could join together to form an enterprise that they themselves would manage on a participatory basis. In these enterprises it was the worker members who signed contracts with the other factors of production, including capital, remunerating them at the market minimum; any profits belonged to the members.

It was in Europe, the cradle of the industrial revolution, that the first cooperatives arose. And the lead in the cooperative movement was quickly taken by England, which was also in the vanguard of the industrial revolution. We have accounts of dairy product cooperatives in France as early as the second half of the eighteenth century, as well as of insurance cooperatives in London and in America (the 'Philadelphia Contributionship for the Insurance of Houses from Loss by Fire', founded by Benjamin Franklin and still in being today). In the nineteenth century cooperatives burgeoned in other European countries in farming, crafts and manufacturing. Consumer cooperatives also arose (the first reported in England in 1828). These were all attempts that had little success, however, because they were unsustainable over time. They lacked the principles of organization that could ensure an effective presence in the market together with the defence of the values of solidarity that they were intended to serve.

Gradually, though, more mature initiatives were consolidated, tracing out 'models' of cooperation that were then imitated throughout the world. The first four, all founded around mid-century, were the consumer cooperative (in England), the labour cooperative (in France), the credit cooperative (in Germany) and the farmers' cooperative (in Denmark). A fifth model, the social cooperative, was created in Italy a century later. Let us examine their salient features (Shaffer, 1999).

2.2   THE MAIN COOPERATIVE MODELS

Rochdale is a small city in Lancashire, the historical centre of the English cotton textile industry. In the 1840s the living conditions of the workers there were miserable indeed. They began working at the age of seven or eight, often continuing to study at evening or Sunday school.

They tried in various ways to improve their lives, with political movements, trade unions and cooperation. But nothing had been truly successful. In 1843 a small group of poor weavers, many short of work and discouraged by earlier failures, met under the leadership of Charles Howart to try once again to improve their lot. This time they launched a subscription for a consumer cooperative that could later be turned to other ends. According to its statute 'the objects and plans of this Society are to form arrangements for the pecuniary benefits and the improvement of the social and domestic conditions of the members'. Strenuous efforts succeeded in raising 28 pounds from 28 persons, and on 21 December 1844 a store was opened in Todd Lane selling small amounts of flour, butter, sugar and oatmeal.

The principles governing the operation of this cooperative store were: (1) sale for cash at fixed prices; (2) end-year rebate proportional to purchases; (3) freedom of purchasing (members were not required to shop only at the co-op); (4) minimum interest on loans; (5) democratic government (one person, one vote; women too could be voting members); (6) ideological neutrality and tolerance. The formula did not take long to become a success. Children could be sent to shop in the co-op, confident that they would not be cheated. Housewives could create a small nest egg with the end-year bonus. Men found a place to meet and discuss their problems. In 1850 members already numbered 600. The next year the store was opened every day. The cooperative then added new sectors (upholstery, butcher shop, shoes, wainscoting, tailor's shop), giving work to many craftsmen. In 1850 the Rochdale District Co-Operative Corn Mill Society was founded so the co-op could procure its own flour. In 1855 a wholesale store was opened, the first of many, and the proliferation of branches began. A library was formed and a meeting hall for men; schools and lectures were promoted, with a fund financed by 2.5 per cent of the operating surplus. Later still the cooperative tried to create production societies, a building co-op and a mutual bank. The Rochdale Society of Equitable Pioneers eventually became a retailing giant, with an elegant, four-storey headquarters building and countless outlets.

The Rochdale model was imitated throughout Britain and gained an ideological hegemony as British economists sustained the principle of 'consumer sovereignty', especially when powerful wholesale societies were formed (the Cooperative Wholesale Society in Manchester in 1863 and the Scottish Cooperative Wholesale Society in 1868). These societies opposed factory workers' sharing in the profits (even in factories linked to the societies themselves), for fear that this would mean higher costs of foodstuffs. This continued to strengthen consumer co-ops but to weaken other forms of cooperation. By 1877 there were no fewer than 1661 British cooperatives with a million members.

The second model was the labour cooperative, which first developed in France. A society of carpenters was formed in Paris as early as 1831, followed by associations of goldsmiths, stonecutters and bakers. In 1848, with the *ateliers nationaux* experiment under Louis Blanc, there were 255 such associations in Paris alone. The first decree on their behalf was passed that same year, creating a fund for workers' co-ops and giving them preference in public works contracting. In 1884 a consultative chamber of workers' production cooperatives was formed with an original group of 29 societies; by 1904 this had grown to 200 (out of a total of 358). Many of these co-ops originated in strikes and the conversion of existing capitalist enterprises into cooperatives. In France these production and labour co-ops also gave rise to experimental labor communities, but eventually these were overcome by the dynamism of consumer, credit and farmers' cooperatives patterned after foreign models.

The third model, from Germany, was the credit union or mutual bank. In 1849, in Anhausen in the Rhine valley, Friedrich Wilhelm Raiffeisen, burgomaster and then entrepreneur, founded the first rural mutual bank, as a partnership, doing local business and lending only to partners. Banks like it spread rapidly, and in 1876 a central German farm credit institute was formed, later to be named the Raiffeisen Bank of Germany. The majority of these banks were religiously inspired, but some were liberal. In 1910 they numbered 15 517, with 2.6 million members. In 1850 Hermann Schulze Delitzsch, judge and member of the national assembly in Berlin, founded the first urban mutual bank, called popular bank. In 1859 there were 111 of these, and in 1864 they formed a central institution. By 1910 they numbered 2103, with a million members. They featured the redistribution of profits to the members, one person, one vote, limits on shareholding, lending at first only to members, then extended to non-members and to a broad range of action. Both Raiffeisen in the countryside and Schultze Delitzsch in the cities subsequently extended cooperation to other fields.

The fourth model, the joint farmers' cooperative, developed in Scandinavia. The Lutheran theologian and bishop Nicolas Friederich Gründtvigts (1783–1872) urged farmers in his diocese to promote farm co-ops and schools. After his death these cooperatives grew considerably in the dairy farming and processing sector that was becoming a Danish specialty. In 1882 the first dairy product cooperative was formed in Hjedding, western Jutland. Starting in 1890 the dairy product co-ops formed associations to export butter, and in 1901 the Cooperative Union of Danish Dairy Producers was founded, followed in 1920 by the Federation of Danish Dairy Producers, which covered virtually the entire industry. The cooperative formula began to spread to other sectors. In 1887 the first cooperative butchery and meat packing operation began in Horsens. In 1890 the Central Office of Cooperative Butchers, followed in 1897 by the Danish Union of Cooperative Butchers. The first livestock export cooperative came in 1898. And in 1899 the Central Cooperative Committee representing all Danish co-ops was founded. Comparable institutions took root in Sweden and Finland.

Our fifth model, finally, is that of social cooperation. It is much more recent than the other four, the fruit of Italian courage and creativity. It was on 23 January 1963 that the first cooperative for social assistance and solidarity was founded in Brescia under the leadership of the Catholic activist Giuseppe Filippini. The society, named after St Joseph, had two distinctive features: bringing people together for primarily spiritual needs (training, education, assistance, recreation, work for the disadvantaged); and acting not only for the benefit of its own members but also for 'others', as Filippini would say at the first conference of the cooperative movement held in Italy in 1977. This pointed to a totally new version of extended mutual cooperation, hardly to be found in the traditional cooperative movement. It implied a multi-stakeholder model of governance, a model in which the representatives of a number of different interest groups all have a say in decisions and a role in the governance structure. Thus the decision-making bodies comprised not only worker-members but also the beneficiaries of the co-ops' services and representatives of the local community. Law 381/1991 instituted the 'social cooperative' within the Italian legal order. The model has been widely emulated and serves as the prototype of the 'social enterprise' in Europe. In 2001 France approved the institution of the 'Société cooperative d'interêt collectif'; in 1999 Spain introduced the 'Cooperativa d'iniciativa social'; in 1998 Portugal established the 'Cooperativa de solidariedade social'; and Greece in 1999 introduced the Limited Liability Social Cooperative.

National legislative action generally accompanied the rise of the cooperative movement, in some cases offering legal recognition of its different nature, in others providing tax allowances in recognition of the social role the co-ops play. Relations between the cooperative movement and organized labour were not always idyllic, especially where the unions were in the hands of political radicals who sought to unhinge the capitalist system and the market along with it. As we already stressed, the cooperative movement does not oppose the market economy, but interprets it differently from capitalism, stressing the central role of people (workers, consumers, savers, local residents who are members of the co-op) rather than that of capital.

2.3 THE COOPERATIVE AS SEEN BY NINETEENTH-CENTURY THINKERS

The European cooperative tradition displays two sharply distinct lines of thought, present from the origins: the French school and the Anglo-Italian. The French movement saw cooperatives as an antidote to the market as interpreted by capitalism. A typical analysis along these lines was that of Charles Gide, who defined the cooperative as an alternative to the capitalistic enterprise:

> There being no limit whatsoever to the number of shares owned, it can happen that some rich capitalist may buy, alone, a much larger part of the firm's equity capital than thousands of small shareholders, reducing the latter's role to zero. The essential character of the cooperative society … is instead that in it capital is not abolished – cooperators are too practical to imagine you can do without capital or obtain it for free – but kept to its true function as an instrument at the service of labour and paid as such. (*La Coopération*, 1900, pp. 98–9).

In this way, the co-op would abolish profit. Another French proponent of this line of thought was Louis Blanc, who coined an even clearer motto: 'The evil is competition, the remedy is [cooperative] association.' In line with the more radical forms of socialist thought, such theoreticians of French cooperation as Charles Fourier called for the abolition of private capital, the elimination of competition and its consequent system of prices. Frédéric Le Play, who founded the 'Société d'Economie Sociale' in 1854 and conducted a vast programme of research designed to foster 'harmony among people cooperating in the same jobs', espoused a utopian ideal in which competition did not exist.

One major figure within British cooperation did share the French approach: Robert Owen (1771–1858), who was the first to use the word 'cooperation' deliberately. He was the founder of a number of complex cooperatives, such as New Harmony in Indiana, New Lanark in England and Orbiston in Scotland. Robert Owen was a strange sort of 'socialist' who did not believe mankind had any inborn aspiration to freedom. Instead he thought man's character could be moulded by changing his living conditions. Assigned by the House of Commons to coordinate the parliamentary commission of inquiry into the application of the Poor Laws, Owen took the chance to draft a report, *Villages of Cooperation*, setting out his radical views on social transformation. The key to his proposal was the cooperative management of the factories, as the core of a new, reconstructed society. Goods would be exchanged on the basis of the amount of labour they contained, and the means of production would be collective property. This shows clearly that ideas which would later be part of Marx's thought circulated before him.

It is easy enough to see that experiments based on this line of thought could not but fail. In 1830 a follower of Owen, William King, founded the Brighton Co-operative Trading Association, grouping more than 300 consumer co-ops. But within the span of a few years, all these initiatives had failed miserably. This line continued in England right down to the time of Sidney and Beatrice Webb, who developed a theory of cooperation based on class struggle (*The Consumers' Cooperative Movement*, 1921).

However the main British cooperative tradition, like the Italian, was quite different, seeing cooperation as a way to 'civilize' the market. George Jacob Holyoake wrote in his *History of the Rochdale Pioneers* (1893):

> What was [the Pioneers] inspiration? They had no learning of the schools, but they had that genius which enters the hearts of honest men ... They put truth first and profit second, believing that principle was the foundation of all honourable profit, and the only honest source of it. It was not dividend which mainly inspired them, for they had never seen it, and they detested the competitive underhandedness by which they saw others acquiring profit ... . Let us keep to their methods and we shall see the day which they desired to see – when principle shall rule in this movement, when the humiliation of hired labour shall cease, when worker as well as purchaser shall share in the profits created, when the penury of the many shall terminate, and the scandalous fortunes of the few be impossible, under the co-operative law of the common interest, inspired by goodwill and governed by equity. (Speech at the store hall, p. 184)

What made the Rochdale co-op work was the idea of charging members the market price for the goods they bought but returning any surplus to them at the end of the year. In the co-ops inspired by Owen, instead, goods were sold below the market price; this illusory idea of helping the members actually drove the co-ops to failure. The Italian scholar Ghino Valenti remarked in 1902:

> Not many words need be wasted to show the radical difference between the communities of Owen and modern cooperative societies. ... Whereas the former abstracted from the mechanism of free competition and aimed to constitute a different social order, the cooperative movement is grafted onto the existing social fabric and intends only to supplement the social body. (Valenti, 1902, p. 33)

It was on this basis that cooperative enterprise gained the favour of eminent British economists, who saw its positive features clearly and understood what set it apart from its philanthropic predecessors. It was not a top-down initiative but the assumption of responsibility for their own fate by working people who wanted to improve their lot by self-help. For John Stuart Mill, the capitalistic enterprise – based on the principle of hierarchy – was a residue of the feudal world. Hence this great liberal thinker's sympathy for the cooperative movement. Together with many other economists of the day, notably John Cairnes, Mill saw cooperation as potentially able to make productive organization compatible with the principle of liberty:

> there is no more certain incident of the progressive change taking place in society, than the continual growth of the principle and practice of cooperation. (Mill, 1852, Book IV, chapter 1, paragraph 2)

Equally celebrated is Mills's further pronouncement:

> The form of association ... which if mankind continues to improve, must be expected, in the end, to predominate is not that which can exist between a capitalist as chief and work-people without a voice in the management, but the association of the labourers themselves on terms of equality, collectively owning the capital with which they carry on their operations and working under managers elected and removable by themselves. (ibid., chapter 7, paragraph 6).

Alfred Marshall – the founder of the neoclassical Cambridge school of economics – went so far as to say that in a cooperative, the worker does not produce for others but for himself, which unleashes an enormous capacity for diligent, high-quality work that capitalism suppresses. There is one ruined product, in the history of the world, so much greater in importance than all the others that it can truly be called the 'wasted product' – the best working capacities of most of the labouring classes. (from his essay *Cooperation*, 1889, p. 7)

The French economist Léon Walras adopted a similar stance, defining 'popular associations' (as the cooperatives were called at first in France) according to their purpose (the creation of capital belonging to all the members indivisibly) and to their means (the regular and continuous setting aside of a portion of the members' income. In *Les associations populaires de consummation, de production et de credit* (1865 [1925], p. 229), he summed this position up. 'Here, in a word, we have the entire system of popular associations – to bring workers to ownership of capital through saving.' And he concluded: 'In fact, the popular associations do exactly what is dictated by political economy.'

Let us turn briefly to America. The first co-ops were simply the transposition of European radicalism. We have mentioned Owen's New Harmony in Indiana. The followers of Fourier founded their 'cooperative phalansteries' in 1840, the most important of which was Brook Farm near Boston. But these experiences were inevitably short-lived. The movement derived new impetus from the thought and work of Aaron Sapiro (1884–1959) and Edwin Nourse (1883–1974), the most important theorists of the cooperative movement in America. Sapiro, a California lawyer, advocated large consumer and farmer cooperatives, but without great success, although he was instrumental in the passage of the Capper-Volstead Act of 1922, the 'Magna Charta' of the US cooperative movement, because he had freed the co-ops from the previously common accusation of anti-competitive conduct. (Actually, the 1914 Clayton Act had already acquitted the cooperatives on this defamatory charge, but it had not offered any concrete support.) Nourse, a Chicago economics professor, favoured small and medium-sized co-ops and a federal structure to enable them to enjoy economies of scale and so to compete with large corporations. Co-founder of the American Institute of Cooperation in 1925, Nourse was also a leader of the International Cooperative Alliance (more below). His influence, not only intellectual but also political, was enormous.

The Italian school, following the civil economics developed in the eighteenth century by Antonio Genovesi, Giacinto Dragonetti, Cesare Beccaria, Pietro Verri and others, and in full concordance with the contemporary work of Mill, Cairnes, Marshall and Walras, saw cooperation as the way to translate civic virtues into practice. The leading nineteenth-century Italian students of cooperation (Fedele Lampertico, Ugo Rabbeno, Luigi Luzzatti, Ghino Valenti, Leone Wollemborg) certainly did not hesitate to criticize the capitalist system, but they never set the cooperative enterprise in conflict with the market economy. On the contrary, they saw the cooperative as an instrument for unleashing the market's full potential. And this same approach can be traced in all the philosophies that inspired the creation of cooperatives in Italy. The first, chronologically, was a particular brand of liberalism[1] (Giuseppe Mazzini, Wollemborg, Luzzatti, Francesco Viganò, Luigi Buffoli), which viewed the cooperative as the place where capital and labour could be reconciled, hence an institution that would favour social peace. In his main work, *The Duties of Man* (1841, and a final edition in 1860), Mazzini wrote, addressing Italian working men:

> Associated labour, the sharing of the fruits of toil ... in proportion to the labour performed and the value of that labour: this is the future of society. Here lies the secret of your emancipation. You once were slaves, then serfs, then wage labourers; provided that you so desire, soon you will be free producers and brothers in association. And this transformation, emancipating you from wage slavery, would at one and the same time enliven and improve the economic state of the country. (1860, pp. 133–4)

The second philosophy was socialism (Andrea Costa, Nullo Baldini, Camillo Prampolini, Giuseppe Massarenti, Antonio Vergnanini), for which cooperatives were the path for the evolutionary – not revolutionary – transformation of capitalism. Ugo Rabbeno wrote that:

> Cooperation, which is the daughter of socialism ... will not follow the path of socialism, taking only that which the latter has that is noble and great ... it will endeavour to realize its own program, following a more modest path, a less adventurous way. (Rabbeno, 1889, p. 154).

Vergnanini affirmed that:

> labour organized on a cooperative basis has declared war on private speculation, not just in order to gained some improvement in the condition of wage

---

[1] This school of thought was named in Italy 'republican', because its members supported a political change of the Italian constitutional setting from monarchy to republic.

labourers but in order to commence, by practical, direct action, to contest the economy's monopoly over society. (Vergnanini, 1907, p. 35).

The third philosophy behind the cooperative movement in Italy, finally, was social Catholicism, with such thinkers as Ercole Chiri, Don Lorenzo Guetti, Luigi Cerutti, Don Luigi Sturzo, Nicolò Rezzara and Giuseppe Toniolo. It centred on the concept of the common good. Toniolo maintained that cooperation 'seems to be called to recreate, in modern guise, the collective ownership of tomorrow. Faced with the present individualism, this is the great social task of the cooperation of the future.' Cooperatives, he believed, would 'raise the agricultural or industrial proletariat to the rank of capitalist'. (Toniolo, 1900 [1951], p. 514).

Don Sturzo repeated that 'unity is strength' (1897), and Don Guetti called for directing everything 'for the common benefit. In your social factories ... it is always "we" that must give luster to the cement, that must strike the eye wherever in the edifice you look' ('Don Mentore ai lettori', *Almanacco Pel 1895*, p. 161).

A specifically Italian trait of the cooperative movement is that despite the variety of philosophical origins no cooperative leader – not even the socialist inspired – ever conceived of the co-op as an anti-market agent. And this common element is what has always made for fruitful dialogue among the diverse traditions, which goes a good way towards explaining the exceptionally great development of the cooperative movement in Italy that is documented below. As Filippo Virgili wrote, 'Cooperative enterprises are economic enterprises, which means that they are not to be confused with charitable or philanthropic associations' (1924, p. 56).

These were the foundations for the international cooperative movement whose features we next explore, before focusing more closely on cooperatives in Italy. As a premise, however, we must first define exactly what is meant by 'cooperative enterprise'.

3. What is a cooperative?

3.1 THE IDENTIFYING FEATURES OF THE COOPERATIVE ENTERPRISE

Today two definitions of cooperative enterprise are current. The most widely used is that of the International Cooperative Alliance (ICA), a non-governmental organization grouping about 230 associations of cooperatives in a hundred countries. Formed in 1895, ICA is the chief moral custodian of the cooperative identity. Its 1995 Co-operative Identity Statement issued in Manchester (after predecessor documents in 1937 and 1966) reads: 'A co-operative is an autonomous association of persons united voluntarily to meet their common economic, social, and cultural needs and aspirations through a jointly-owned and democratically-controlled enterprise.'

The Congress of Manchester laid down seven principles for cooperatives. The last is new, but the first six were the same ones – slightly reworded – that the original Rochdale Society of Equitable Pioneers had adopted in 1844. That the fundamental principles have remained unchanged for over a century and a half is remarkable in itself. Let us now review them.

1. Voluntary and open membership. Cooperatives are voluntary organizations and enterprises, open to all persons able to use their services and willing to accept the responsibilities of membership, without gender, social, racial, political or religious discrimination. This is known in the movement as the 'open door' principle.
2. Democratic member control. Unlike capitalist firms, in which shareholder votes are weighted, not counted, both in primary cooperatives and at other levels the cooperative movement adopts the rule 'one member, one vote'. That is, in general or at board meetings all members have equal voting rights.
3. Member economic participation. Members contribute equitably –

not necessarily equally – to, and democratically control, the capital of their cooperative. At least part of that capital is usually the common property of the cooperative. If the by-laws so provide, members may receive limited compensation on capital subscribed as a condition of membership. The reason for the limit to such compensation is to avert the risk that as it proceeds the cooperative may change its *raison d'être*. The net operating surplus will be allocated in part to reserves, part of which at least should be indivisible; in part to benefits for members in proportion to their transactions with the cooperative; and in part to support for other activities approved by the membership – typically, external mutual cooperation.

4. Autonomy and independence. Cooperatives are autonomous, self-help organizations controlled by their members. If for some reason they enter into agreements with other organizations or raise capital from external sources, they must do so on terms that ensure democratic control by their members and maintain their cooperative autonomy.

5. Education, training and information. Cooperatives provide not only training but also education for their members, elected representatives, managers and employees (the original Rochdale principles mandated that 2.5 per cent of the yearly surplus was to go to research and member education). They may also inform the general public about the nature and the mission of cooperation.

6. Cooperation among cooperatives. Cooperative action is not limited to action within each single enterprise. That is, cooperatives serve their members most effectively and strengthen the cooperative movement by working together through local, national, regional and international structures.

7. Concern for community. This is a new principle added by the Manchester Congress. In this view, cooperatives must work for the sustainable development of their communities through policies approved by their members. A practical expression of the cooperative movement's marked social orientation is the rule adopted by Italian cooperatives in 1992 to allocate 3 per cent of their annual surplus to mutual aid funds.

The second definition of cooperative enterprise is that of the US Department of Agriculture, which in 1987 defined a cooperative as 'an enterprise owned and controlled by its users, which distributes benefits based on the use they make of it'. Defining members as 'owner-users' implies that those who 'use' the co-op (the members) participate in financing it and thus own it. Members must supply at least part of the cooperative's capital, and the contribution of each is in proportion to the use they make of the cooperative. And this is what engenders the common ownership of the enterprise. The term 'user control', for that matter, implies that the members govern the cooperative both directly and indirectly through their representatives on the board of directors. Clearly, in the cooperative there can be no separation between owner-ship and control.

Going by this US definition, there is the possibility of exception, in some circumstances, to the 'one member, one vote' principle. Voting rights may be made proportional to the volume of business the members do with the cooperative – but never, in any case, to the capital subscribed. In US practice democratic control of the co-op is ensured by tying voting rights to effective participation in the life of the organiza-tion, not to the simple head count. This aspect is further reinforced by the principle that the benefits are to be distributed on the basis of the use made. Members thus share the benefits as well as the costs and risks, in proportion to their patronage. They thus have an incentive for close rela-tions with the co-op.

The nature of the benefit (better prices for goods and services; better and above all more secure jobs and working conditions; guaranteed market outlets for products; capitalizing on one's services) defines the type of cooperative. Thus a worker cooperative is one in which all or some of the enterprise's workers are members. In the user cooperative (consumption, housing) members are consumers or other users. In the support cooperative (farmers, credit, retailing) members are self-employed workers or firms that sell their products to the co-op and acquire the goods and services it supplies. Finally, the practice of membership rebates is favoured by the rule that no more than 8 per cent of the operating surplus can be allocated to remuneration of capital subscribed by the members. The rationale for this rule is that the provi-sion of capital depends on the member's relationship with the co-op, which is formed in order to produce benefits for members, not return to capital invested.

As we see, the two definitions are largely convergent, though with readily appreciable differences. We shall examine the latter further on. For now, the point is that what stands at the origin of the cooperative – regardless of sector – is the primary if not necessarily exclusive need to serve the common needs of the members. The central objective of a cooperative, then, is to maximize the remuneration of the member's contribution – whether it is labour, asset conferrals or patronage of the co-op's goods and services is indifferent; not, as in the capitalist firm, the return on capital invested (Bonin and Putterman, 1987; Bonin et al., 1993).

3.2   SUPPLEMENTARY ELEMENTS

Over the years these common basic principles have been supplemented by others reflecting national realities. Referring especially – but not exclusively – to Italy, we can mention several: variability of the cooperative's equity (the member can always opt out, redeeming their quota); the assignment of the co-op's assets, in case of winding up, to funds for the promotion of cooperatives or, alternatively, to the state; a standard clause prohibiting the transformation of the cooperative into some other form of enterprise; and the possibility for the co-op to have relations with third parties. The sense of these additional rules is readily seen. Variable capital is essentially a way to eliminate or at least greatly reduce exit barriers; without it the primary principle of 'voluntary and open membership' would be nullified, de facto. The rules mandating the assignment of assets and prohibiting transformation are clearly intended to counter opportunistic actions by members, who could otherwise decide – with no economic justification – to wind up the co-op and divide its assets among themselves. Finally, from the very beginning, in order to enable cooperatives to attain a critical volume of business they were allowed to have dealings with non-members – worker co-ops employing non-member workers, consumer co-ops selling to non-member customers, mutual banks taking deposits from and lending to non-members, farmers' co-ops buying from non-member producers. The Italian company law reform of 2003, with specific reference to this rule, introduced the distinction between 'prevalently mutualistic' and 'prevalently non-mutualistic' cooperatives. We shall explore the significance of these expressions further on.

We are now in a position to see why the cooperative member can never be likened to the capitalist shareholder. As Alberto Zevi (2005) notes, the former is, de facto, a user of the co-op, with quite limited rights (they cannot make dispositions concerning the indivisible reserves; if the co-op is wound up they cannot benefit from any capital gain; the usufruct right, never transferable or negotiable, remains theirs only as long as they maintain their mutualistic relationship with the co-op). The capitalist shareholder is, in a word, the owner. So we can see that the ultimate discriminant between cooperative and capitalist corporation is that observed by George J. Holyoake, an apostle of cooperation and the first important historian of the cooperative movement: 'Capitalists hired wage labourers, paid the market price of labour, and appropriated all the gain. Cooperative labour proposes to hire capital, pay the market price for it, and appropriate all the gains' (Holyoake, 1893, p. 28).

Interestingly, in *The Wealth of Nations* (1776) Adam Smith anticipated that the division of labour did not, per se, preclude labour's 'hiring' capital and thus controlling the enterprise. In short, we can say that the cooperative is an economic agent combining, inseparably, two distinct dimensions: associationism, in which different people with their own specific needs but sharing a social motivation come together freely for purposes that each individually could not attain, and entrepreneurship, which establishes that the method, the way to attain those aims, is the creation of an enterprise, a stable organization of productive activity directed to the market. The mutual aid society and mutual societies in general – the precursors of the cooperative movement – lack this second element, which is lacking in today's charitable or voluntary associations as well. The capitalistic firm lacks the first element. The cooperative, to arise and above all to flourish, needs both the strong drive to associationism and a functioning market. This is why the cradle of the cooperative movement could only have been in Europe, where since the era of civic humanism in the fifteenth century and with the decisive impetus of the Enlightenment (not so much French as Scottish and Italian Enlightenment) these two elements found fertile soil. At the same time, we can also understand why, as we saw in the previous chapter, the first successful cooperatives were consumer co-ops. It is in the sphere of consumption, in fact, that association and entrepreneurship are most readily reconciled and thus most easily combined.

3.3   WHY ARE THERE COOPERATIVES AT ALL?

Now that we know what a cooperative enterprise is, and what its distinctive features are, we can address the next question: why should such enterprises exist at all? Put another way, why are there rational economic agents who find it in their interest to create a co-op instead of a capital-ist firm? Basically, there are two approaches to answering this question. According to the demand-side approach, cooperatives arise in response to the inability of private corporations and public enterprises to meet certain social needs or resolve certain crisis situations. That is, coopera-tives are viewed as the remedy, either temporary or durable, for the familiar 'market failures' and 'government failures' – all those cases in which neither market logic nor the logic of the state can attain socially desirable objectives. Note, though, that they are always the remedy for someone else's failings. This approach, still the prevalent one especially among economists, makes the cooperative in any case an exception to the rule. A careful reading of most of the literature soon uncovers the secret thought of these economists, namely that if we ever managed to eliminate or greatly attenuate the negative effects of externalities, asym-metrical information, incomplete contracts and so on, there would be no need for cooperation. That is to say, the more closely the market comes to the ideal-type of perfect competition and the more the state manages to rid itself of bureaucratic excesses, internalities and rent seeking, the less need there is for co-ops.

The supply-side approach turns this vision upside down. In this view, the cooperative is formed and kept alive by the decision of people who put positive liberty – *libertas electionis* or 'freedom to' – at the top of their scale of values. Unlike 'freedom from' – absence of constraint, or *libertas indifferentiae* – 'freedom to' is liberty with a view to an end (Lukes, 1997). In our case this end is the power to control the enterprise one is engaged in. The employee of a capitalist firm enjoys 'freedom from', insofar as in a market economy no one is compelled to take a job, but they do not have the 'freedom to' exercise full autonomy once they have signed the contract. What underlies the formation of cooperatives, then, is the irrepressible yearning for positive liberty, whether or not there are unsatisfied social needs or situations of special economic uncertainty (Birchell, 1994).

We ourselves subscribe to this second point of view, which, may we point out, in no way excludes the idea that the passion for 'freedom to' can be combined and bolstered by other aims, such as intergenerational solidarity, one's legitimate personal interest and more. Instead, the supply-side approach basically says that the cooperative form is the most advanced mode, today, of imagining our labour as an opportunity for self-realization and not just simply a factor of production. Alfred Marshall's 'substitution principle' clearly suggested that labour is a highly peculiar 'input', because it is at once the means of production of goods and the means of production of human personality. Yet the abundant economic literature comparing capitalist and cooperative enterprise never considers this aspect. Labour is never treated as anything but an 'input', an argument of the production function. So it can come as no surprise at all, as we shall see in Chapter 6, that the conclusions generated by these models – technically sophisticated as they may be – almost always tell in favour of the capitalist company, by the standards of comparative efficiency. For the usual notion of efficiency, notoriously, pays no heed whatever to the formation of human character. Only a reductive vision of work, in fact, can see labour-as-toil (typical of the employee) as equivalent to labour-as-action (typical of the co-op member-worker).

It would be interesting to probe the reasons why, starting towards the end of the nineteenth century, the supply-side school was abandoned for the demand-side. The architects of this change certainly include the celebrated Italian economists Maffeo Pantaleoni and Vilfredo Pareto, whose pessimistic view of cooperation seriously limited subsequent theoretical discussion. In their framework, in fact, the decision to join a cooperative was attributed exclusively to a calculation of economic self-interest, just as the American management expert Chester Barnard proclaimed: 'Cooperation means business' and 'business is business'. Adopting the assumption – which is, let us repeat, only an assumption – that all economic agents are purely self-interested *homines oeconomici*, these writers cannot even conceive of the idea that some people may want to work in a certain way, without hierarchy or command, and for the realization of certain ideals.

In the twentieth century, economists were so much concerned with analysing capitalist markets and modes of production that they never granted more than passing attention to the cooperative form of enterprise. In fact, the very first formal theoretical model comparing capitalist and cooperative enterprise was developed by an American scholar, Benjamin Ward, and it did not come until 1958. In management science too there has never been systematic or adequate investment in cooperative management. Even today, organization theory still 'sees' the cooperative only insofar as it deviates from the capitalist model. The latter, that is, is taken as the ideal-type, whose management and governance rules need to be 'adjusted' to accommodate the cooperative. This explains the frequently observed identity of the modus operandi of managers in capitalist and in cooperative enterprises. The lack of a comprehensive, robust body of organizational doctrine designed specifically for co-ops explains the cases of degenerations of cooperatives. Simply to transplant the organizational patterns and rules of operation designed for the capitalist corporation into a co-op is to undermine the latter's identity and condemn it to eventual disappearance (Stiglitz, 1994).

The point is that it is simply not true that corporate management techniques are neutral, that is, indifferent with respect to the type of enterprise. And the reason is clear. There are two main types of motive for economic action. One is teleological – you do something to obtain the best possible outcome given the circumstances – and stems from particular passions, such as acquisitiveness. The other is non-instrumental – you do something for its intrinsic meaning, not just for the final outcome – and springs from such values as equity, reciprocity and love of liberty. Both motives are to be found, in differing proportions, in all the agents within the market. Some set the highest priority on working in an enterprise based on mutual trust, sense of equity and personal respect. And there are also those who prefer anonymous, impersonal work, for whom compliance with the law is perfectly sufficient for the efficient operation of a firm. For them, the sole form of social life they seek is the contractual model, meaning that the only social ties that are justified are those that best satisfy individual interests. Clearly, given a real (not virtual) choice, the former type of person will choose the cooperative, the latter the capitalistic firm. How, in this case, can one imagine that the quality of the work environment and, more generally, organizational models are the same in the two types of enterprise? Quite simply, as Chapter 7 shows, we do not think you can.

3.4   ON THE COOPERATIVE IDENTITY

The central question is this: where to place the *fundamentum divisionis* (ultimate discriminant) between the cooperative and the capitalist enterprise? By now, we are familiar with the factors characterizing the co-op: democratic governance, mutual exchange, unavailability of indivisible reserves to individual members, the open door principle, external cooperation and more. But where do these factors come from? In other words, what is the summary principle from which these particular characteristics spring?

We must start from the consideration that economic action, any economic action, is always common action. 'Common' action is any action that cannot be carried out without the deliberate contribution of more than one agent. On close inspection, the division of labour makes all economic actions common actions, which are distinguished by three elements. First, all those involved must be aware of what they are doing; the mere meeting or coming together of several individuals is not a common action. Second, each individual participant is the author and retains responsibility for what they do. This is what sets common action apart from collective action, in which individual identity vanishes, along with personal responsibility for actions. Third, the participants join forces for the same objective. The interaction of a number of persons within a given context does not constitute common action if they are pursuing different or conflicting aims. Thus an economic enterprise, inasmuch as it has all three elements, is itself a common action.

Common actions themselves differ, however, according to the subject of their 'commonness', which may relate either to means or to ends. In the one case the enterprise will be capitalistic and interpersonal relations will be governed by contract. In a contract, it is true, both parties work for its realization, but they pursue different and often conflicting ends. Just think of a sales contract between vendor and purchaser, or an employment contract. In the other case, when what is held in common is ends, you have the cooperative enterprise. Note the difference between a situation in which everyone agrees that each is to pursue their own end (as in the capitalistic firm) and one in which a common end is agreed on. This is the same difference as that between a local public good and a common good. In the latter, but not the former, the advantage to each from its use cannot be separated from the advantage drawn by others. That is, each party's interest in the common good is realized together with that of the other parties, not against them as in the private good or regardless of them, as in the public good. Where public is opposed to private, common is opposed to one's own. Common is that which is not only one's own, nor indistinctly everyone's. So a cooperative is a form of enterprise in which the relations between members are directed to a common end: mutual aid is attained through the exercise of a specific economic activity.

Economically speaking, what consequences stem from this distinction? The main one is that when the action in common stops at means, the basic problem to be solved is coordination of many people. Management science has provided for this in totally sufficient fashion, first with the pioneering work of Frederick W. Taylor (1911) and then with Herbert Simon after World War II. But when what is in common extends to ends and purposes, the problem is one of cooperation. In formal terms, a problem of coordination arises from the strategic inter-dependence of a number of different persons. In fact, if there were no division of labour, there would be no problem of coordination. At the same time, the characteristics of the production process themselves determine the mode of coordination, as in the assembly line. A problem of cooperation, in contrast, arises from axiological interdependence, that is, the fact that the members consciously pursue the common end. This implies that the behaviour of each depends on their expectations about the intentions – not just the behaviour – of the others. Thomas Schelling has written, most aptly, that the problem of cooperation is to bring about a 'meeting of minds'.

How can the problem of cooperation be resolved? Bratman (1999) offers a convincing answer in three conditions: mutual responsiveness, commitment to the joint activity and commitment to mutual support. The first means that each participant in the common action must consider the intentions of the others to be important, worthy of respect, and be sure that this applies to all – that is, it is not enough for the members to intend to undertake the same action, they must want to do it together. The second means that, albeit possibly for different reasons, each member must be committed to a joint activity and be sure that the others are as well, implying that it is impossible to quantify the specific contribution of each to the joint product. The third, finally, means that each pledges to help the others in their efforts so that the end result is the best possible.

It is worth observing that this mutual support must be provided during the joint activity, not outside it or when it is terminated. So mutual support is neither self-interested nor altruistic and disinterested. As there is a joining of interests, in providing support to others you are continuing to pursue your own interest. In other words, just because they are concerned with their own welfare the cooperative member is inter-ested in the well-being of the others (Dworkin, 1992). This is the specific interpretation of the principle of reciprocity that the cooperative practices under the name of 'mutuality'. The principle of reciprocity runs like this: I give or do something for you so that you in turn can give or do for others, perhaps for me. By contrast, the exchange of equiva-lents runs: I give you something on condition that in exchange you give me something of equivalent value. The principle of pure altruism (phil-anthropy) runs: I give you something on condition that you give me nothing; in fact, I don't even want to know who you are. Philanthropy, naturally, is perfectly compatible with capitalistic action (as in the many cases of corporate charitable donations), but the latter does not tolerate the principle of reciprocity (Bruni, 2006).

In short, the discriminant between the two types of enterprise lies in the difference between 'acting' and 'doing'. A person 'acts' when they perform an action for a purpose they themselves have chosen. A person who 'does', who 'operates', who performs an action ordered by others, whose purpose they may not know and for which in any case, even if they do know, they are not responsible. So where the employee 'operates' and is accountable only for their own task, the cooperative member 'acts' and is thus accountable for the purpose of their work (Zamagni, 2005).

4. The development of cooperation in the world

4.1 THE RISE OF THE INTERNATIONAL COOPERATIVE MOVEMENT

Very early on, in 1835, Robert Owen founded an Association of All Classes and All Nations designed to bring together all the groups practising cooperation. The realization of this idea, however, came very slowly indeed. An attempt was made in 1867 to organize a first international meeting of cooperators in Paris, in concomitance with the Exposition Universelle, but the French government would not allow it, for fear of disorders. Other attempts were made, but the century had practically run out before 200 delegates from 13 countries could meet for a week in London, in August 1895, to emerge with the foundation of the International Cooperative Alliance. Nine of the 13 countries were European, and the other four (the USA, Argentina, Australia and India) were permeated by European culture. The ICA, which soon evolved into an association of cooperative federations (single cooperatives could not join directly) acted mainly to defend the cooperative identity in its congresses and publications – not without difficulty, given the wars that set member nations in conflict with one another and the presence of authoritarian regimes that opposed the very essence of cooperation, that is, its profoundly democratic roots.

The ICA eventually had to grapple with the divisive question of admission for organizations that were nominally cooperatives but actually state-run bodies under Soviet control. The difficult decision eventually made was not to expel them, but the ICA had to defend itself against the attempts of the Soviet bloc representatives to dominate the association. During the 1930s the number of member federations plunged with the spread of dictatorship throughout Europe (not just the Soviet Union but also Italy, Germany, a number of East European countries, Portugal and Spain). The Alliance nevertheless had the courage, at its Paris Congress in 1937, to reaffirm the democratic principles of the movement: 'In whatever type of economic system, the cooperative movement requires total independence of action as the foundation of its principles and rejects any attempt to establish political control over its activity.'

Towards the end of World War II the ICA appealed to its members in the non-belligerent countries to raise resources for the reconstruction of cooperatives in the war-torn nations of Europe. It raised $300 000 (equivalent to $3 million at today's prices), testifying to the solidarity characterizing the international movement. In 1946 the ICA was granted advisor status to the United Nations, like such organizations as the International Labour Organization (ILO) and the Food and Agriculture Organization (FAO), and began a process of diversification by sector and geographical area, permitting a more practical approach to problems of organization as well as of principle. In 1982 the ICA central office was moved from London to Geneva, and work began on the idea of a special fund to develop co-ops in the poor countries where their growth was halting at best. The ICA, with its sector and geographical units, thus became an essential economic, political and cultural representative of the world cooperative movement. At the Manchester Congress in 1995, as we have seen, the cooperative identity was concisely reformulated (Shaffer, 1999).

Today the ICA groups 227 federations of cooperatives in 91 countries all over the world, with 800 million members (180 million in China, 210 million in India) and 100 million people employed. Europe alone counts 267 000 co-ops in 37 countries, with membership of 163 million and a workforce of 5.5 million. The countries where the movement is strongest are Finland, Sweden, Ireland and Canada, where half the population is a member of a cooperative; followed by Norway, Denmark, France, Japan and – surprisingly – the USA, where more than a third of the population are co-op members. In many other countries, including Italy, membership reaches at least a fourth of the population. No economic sector is untouched, but the broadest presence is registered in farming and food processing, retailing, where consumer co-ops are flanked by powerful retailers' co-ops, and banking and insurance. Housing cooperatives – building societies – have also been created everywhere but are often not adequately reflected in the statistics, because they involve fixed term cooperation, forming organizations that are practically always dissolved with the member's acquisition of the home.

More recently the ICA has completed an innovative project to identify the world's 300 largest cooperatives (Global 300), and the results are interesting indeed. These 300 cooperative enterprises have total sales of $1 trillion, with 33 per cent in farming and food processing, 25 per cent in wholesale or retail trade and 22 per cent in insurance. They come from 28 different countries: 15 in Europe, four in the Americas, six in Asia, plus Australia, New Zealand and Israel. The five countries with the largest cooperative sales volume are, in order, France, Japan, the USA, Germany and the Netherlands; those with the largest number of co-ops in the Global 300 are the USA, France, Germany, Italy and the Netherlands; and those where co-ops account for the largest portion of national income are Finland, New Zealand, Switzerland, the Netherlands and Norway.

In 2003 the European Union issued its Statute for a European Cooperative Society, an indispensible instrument towards the possible unity of cooperatives in Europe. In February 2009 the European Parliament passed a resolution on social economy that asked the Commission 'to defend the social economy's concept of a "different approach to entrepreneurship", which is not driven mainly by the profit motive but by social benefit' (8) and advocates a more adequate legal and statistical recognition of the Third Sector, including mutual societies, associations and foundations, in view of the fact that 'social economy enterprises and organizations help to strengthen the entrepreneurial spirit, facilitate better democratic functioning of the business world, incorporate social responsibility and promote the active social integration of vulnerable categories' (18) beside helping 'to rectify three major labour market imbalances: unemployment, job instability and the social and labour exclusion' (20).

We proceed now to give an account of the evolution of the cooperative movement in some of the countries where it is more established, leaving the case of Italy for the next chapter.

4.2   FRANCE

We saw that France was the first country where worker cooperatives arose; in the second half of the nineteenth century these were joined by consumer co-ops, farmers' co-ops – still very strong today – and credit unions, especially rural credit unions. In 1894 local and regional agricultural credit unions formed a central organization, Crédit Agricole, which was flanked by cooperative banks and other mutual banks. Since then French credit cooperation has grown enormously, and in 2001 it accounted for 57 per cent of the country's total deposits and 37 per cent of its lending. Crédit Agricole freed itself completely from government controls in 1988 and obtained stock exchange listing for its holding company – wholly owned at first by the regional credit unions, which later sold part of their holdings but retained a majority stake – in order to conduct major economic transactions (such as the acquisition of Crédit Lyonnais) nationally and internationally. Today Crédit Agricole is the largest banking group in France and one of the largest in the world, and non-profit mutual insurance societies account for more than half of the French insurance market.

Consumer cooperatives have not been equally successful. The process of consolidation of small co-ops was completed after World War II, but this was not accompanied by a strategy for modernization of the sales network, which continues to consist mainly of small shops; the few cooperative hypermarkets founded never became profitable and had to be severely downsized (they were eventually sold to private corporations). The causes for this failure were many: the movement's inability to develop a rigorous management structure; the difficulties in relations between local and national cooperative structures, with the local co-ops showing little inclination to use central purchasing services; and the undifferentiated structure for managing tiny outlets and hypermarkets. In the 1990s the presence of consumer co-ops in France consisted mainly of four regional cooperatives that arose from the progressive merging of smaller units: Coop Atlantique, Coop Normandie Picardie, Coop Alsace and Les coopérateurs de Champagne. In 2002 these four groups ran 15 hypermarkets, 75 supermarkets, 213 discount supermarkets and over 500 neighbourhood shops. They are multichannel companies, depending on high quality and strong territorial roots, expressed in members' involvement in cultural and recreational activities.

French cooperative organizations, then, were numerous and widespread. They were grouped into regional and then national federations, with the substantial (and sometimes cumbersome) support of the state. The Groupement national de la coopération was founded as the overarching organization. Today it counts 19 million members, including 12 million members of credit unions and 3.4 million members of retail cooperatives (particularly strong, with 15 076 outlets, 128 000 workers, with a leading role in such retailing sectors as sporting goods, optics, do-it-yourself and foods). Another characteristic of the French cooperative movement was the formation, in the late nineteenth and early twentieth centuries, of school co-ops. Now there are more than 50 000 such co-ops, grouped into 101 provincial associations with 4.5 million students.

In France, then, despite some shortcomings, the cooperative movement covers a broad range of economic sectors and regions. In this it resembles those of Italy and of Scandinavia (the situation in Finland is described below); it differs from these, however, in its relatively close relationship with the state apparatus (Defourny and Spear, 1995).

4.3   FINLAND

Finland is the most 'cooperative' country in the world, outdoing even the rest of Scandinavia. The movement began in the second half of the nineteenth century in farming and prospered, giving rise in 1899 to the Confederation of Finnish Cooperatives, Pellervo (deriving from the Finnish world for 'field'), grouping 390 agricultural co-ops at first. The founder members included university professors, industrialists and bankers who believed that cooperatives would serve not only to spread material well-being but also to increase popular self-esteem and mass participation in the movement for economic and political liberation from the Russian yoke. Two apostles of cooperation devoted their entire lives to the movement: Hannes Gebhard, long the head of Pellervo, and his wife Hedvig, who was also a member of the Finnish Parliament (she would die in 1961 at the age of 96). In 1902 a cooperative bank, Okobank, was founded. Consumer co-ops followed; the largest of these, Sok, was founded in 1904 and now includes a large purchasing consortium (Hankkija Maatalous Oy), forestry industry cooperatives (Metsäliitto) and mutual insurance societies. Today cooperatives account for nearly all agricultural activity, a third of lumbering and forestry, a third of credit business, 40 per cent of retailing, 40 per cent of insurance and more. The three pillars underpinning it are network structure, special legislation and coordination provided by sector leader co-ops.

4.4   SWITZERLAND

In Switzerland too the cooperative movement had already achieved some success by the mid-nineteenth century, and the first national cooperative conference in 1853 saw the participation of 34 consumer co-ops.

Agricultural, electricity, water, credit, housing and worker cooperatives would follow. The Swiss Union of Consumer Cooperatives, the country's first really large cooperative organization, was founded in 1890, but it was not until after World War II that the movement was coordinated, with the institution of a single logo in 1960. In that year there were some 400 consumer co-ops with 3320 retail outlets, but a series of mergers brought the number of co-ops down to 40, then 18, then 14. In 2001 the final merger was completed, forming the new Coop society, which is broadly diversified and controls 15 per cent of the Swiss market. Together with retailer cooperatives in Belgium (Coloruyt), France (Leclerc), Germany (Rewe) and Italy (Conad), in 2006 it founded the first European co-op, Coopernic, which has 17 498 outlets and 100 billion in sales.

However, Coop is not the only Swiss consumer cooperative. There is also Migros, larger still, whose origin was somewhat atypical. Migros was founded as a public limited company in 1925 by Gottlieb Duttweiler, a merchant with progressive ideas and a strong sense of social responsibility. In 1941 he transformed it into a cooperative. Today it is Switzerland's leading retail organization, the second largest cooperative in Europe (after Crédit Agricole) and the seventh largest in the world, with 2 million members and 80 000 employees. Mutual credit is also important, with 405 banks that together form the third-leading Swiss banking group, with 1.4 million members and 19 per cent of total bank deposits.

4.5 GERMANY

The German cooperative movement, with its powerful base in mutual credit, developed significantly up until World War I. It was closely linked to the labour and socialist movement, but not to that alone. In 1913 Germany had over 35 000 co-ops with 6 million members. Their expansion continued in the Weimar period, and by 1933 there were 50 000 co-ops with 9 million members. The Nazi regime put an end to this, dismantling all of the movement's central structures and subjecting the co-ops to direct government control; membership plummeted. World War II completed the job with the physical destruction of the movement's property. The movement had to start up from scratch after the war. This new beginning adhered to the same principle that governed the rest of the economy in West Germany, namely 'decentralization' in the name of democracy, to underscore the difference from the centralism of the Nazi dictatorship. At a time when the European economy was strengthening and emulating the American model of large corporations, this formula was not likely to make the cooperative movement flourish.

Nevertheless, cooperative credit – perhaps the strongest of the movement's historical roots – succeeded in reorganizing, forming a single central institute (Deutsche Genossenschaftsbank, or DG Bank) in 1949, and in 1972 a single national organization, the Bundesverband der Deutschen Volksbanken und Raiffeisenbanken (BVR). The base remained the regional structures. Later some regional organizations merged, and then themselves merged with DG Bank, in 2001 giving rise to the Deutsche Zentral Genossenschaftsbank (DZ Bank). Only one regional bank remained (the WGZ), and it has still not agreed to merge with the rest. Today German cooperative banks number more than 1300, with 14 500 branches and 15 million members, and account for 19 per cent of German bank deposits and 12 per cent of lending.

The strategy for consumer co-ops, in contrast, proved inadequate. After the inauguration of the first self-service store in 1949 and a process of concentration of small co-ops to form more solid organizations, in 1968 a supermarket with 10 000 square metres of floor space was opened in the outskirts of Cologne, followed by five more. Between 1969 and 1972 German consumer cooperatives underwent a radical overhaul with the creation of a central management organization (Bund Deutscher Konsumgenossenschaften GmbH), which in subsequent years renewed the retail network, intensified concentration and then began a campaign to transform the co-ops into public limited companies to facilitate financing. This change largely removed management activities from membership control. In 1975 the process of regionalization was well advanced; the 11 largest regional cooperatives accounted for more than 70 per cent of total sales by consumer cooperatives.

The transition to a nationwide dimension began to be planned in the early 1980s, and a strategy of expansion was undertaken starting in 1985 which, sustained by generous finance from the banks, was intended to win specialized markets. But these plans, and the resort to bank debt, concealed serious operational problems that management had kept hidden for too long. When they emerged in 1989, the only way out was bankruptcy. Today Germany has 85 consumer cooperatives, most of them small, and fewer than a million members. Three groupings are medium-sized (Coop Dortmund, Coop Schleswig Holstein and Coop Nord Bayern). During the 1990s the most dynamic was Coop Schleswig. Its presence in its home region expanded, and by the end of the decade it counted 77 supermarkets and 26 hypermarkets, with a social identity based on quality, regional roots and social activities.

All in all, despite its 22 million members and its significant presence in agriculture (3200 co-ops), in services and small business (1000 co-ops) and in housing (2000 co-ops), the German cooperative movement no longer has the economic power that had distinguished it before the advent of the Nazi regime.

4.6 SPAIN

Here too, the cooperative movement arose in the nineteenth century, when a series of powerful regional organizations were created. A nationwide federation did not come into being until 1928. The Franco dictatorship overturned the balance that had been achieved. The movement just barely survived, and then recovered only very partially, remaining marginal with about 20 000 cooperatives and just 4 million members. Spanish cooperation is known to the rest of the world not for its national organization, but rather for the presence of a unique cooperative experience, Mondragòn (Williams, 2007). The foundation of the first cooperatives in the Basque town that lends its name to what is now a powerful economic group stemmed from the activities of a priest, José Maria Arizmendiarrieta, who was made chaplain and then parish priest of Mondragòn in the 1940s. In 1943 he opened a vocational school for young people, and 1956 saw the founding of the first co-op, Fagor, which made stoves and radiators. It was the first of many, and by the end of the 1960s the Mondragòn co-ops numbered 41. They were organized and financed by a bank, Caja Laboral, that had been founded in 1959, the same year that the collective insurance company Lagun-Aro was activated. In 1969 a retailing society, Eroski, was formed. But unlike those anywhere else, even though its field is retailing, Eroski is not a consumer but a worker co-op.

Ninety per cent of the Mondragòn co-ops' dividends are retained, in order to capitalize co-ops. The original nucleus grew towards self-sustaining organization with the creation of a Polytechnical School in 1962 and a research centre (Ikerlan) in 1974, both of which were incorporated into the University of Mondragòn in 1997. The need to reorganize led in 1984 to the constitution of a group governed by a congress, which linked together consortia of cooperatives in nearby areas. But very soon (in 1991) this organization gave way to a new structure, based on product group divisions, with central departments responsible for finance, innovation, internationalization and cooperative identity. In this way, Mondragòn has been able to face the challenges of globalization (Reed and McMurtry, 2009). Today the Mondragòn group counts some 80 000 workers, 80 per cent of whom are members, and is Spain's seventh largest industrial group in terms of sales and third largest in terms of staff size. Mondragòn is Europe's fourth leading cooperative, after Crédit Agricole, Migros and the Cooperative Group in England.

Despite its undeniable success, with the sole exception of the Eroski retailing chain which has achieved a certain degree of geographical diversification, the Mondragòn group remains an enclave in the Basque country, where it accounts for 8.3 per cent of local output and 14 per cent of employment. Its capacity to move into related economic sectors or neighbouring geographical areas is scant.

4.7 USA

In the second half of the nineteenth century there was an extremely intense American cooperative movement in all fields, including such innovative industries as telephones, electricity and water supply. Many states passed laws regulating cooperatives, and in the 1920s the federal government also enacted legislation. Johns Hopkins University published a history of cooperation in the USA in 1888, testifying to the movement's great early dynamism. A series of federations, institutes and industry associations were formed. Shortly after World War II the strongest sector was farmers' cooperatives, with over 7 million members, but they contracted along with the relative importance of farming in the economy. Today US farmers' co-ops still have 4 million members and account for a third of US agricultural output.

In the credit sector, in contrast, US cooperation has scored success after success, with 84 million members and some 10 000 credit unions in 2005. The other two sectors in which the cooperative movement is powerful are insurance, with 1000 mutual societies administering $80 billion in premiums, and electricity, with 900 co-ops serving 37 million customers. Consumer cooperatives have retained only a niche role, such as that of REI, which markets sporting goods and outdoor equipment and gear, with 3 million members and 82 outlets.

Overall, some 120 million Americans (well over a third of the total population) belong to at least one cooperative. Some co-ops are huge (29 have annual sales of a billion dollars or more). A national cooperative organization was founded in 1916 as the Cooperative League of America. In 1922, when it incorporated the rest of the nation's cooperatives, its name was changed to Cooperative League of the USA. In 1985 it changed its name again, to National Cooperative Business Association (NCBA). The NCBA actively supports cooperatives. In the 1940s the Cooperative League designed programmes to support cooperatives in the war-torn countries of Europe, followed by programmes in the less developed countries. The Cooperative League promoted a number of support institutions, such as the National Cooperative Bank, founded in the 1970s and now doing business for more than a billion dollars a year. In the 1990s the organization persuaded Congress to enact a programme of support for rural co-ops (Ben-Ner et al., 2000).

4.8 CANADA

Cooperatives started in Canada in the middle of the nineteenth century first in the consumer and farmer sectors. Marketing cooperatives and creameries were established in many areas of the country and grew without interruptions; today they have become powerful corporations, accounting for over 40 per cent of total farm cash receipts. The first Credit Union was founded in 1900 by Alphonse Desjardins, the prototype of a large French speaking movement that has today, together with its English speaking counterpart (the Canadian Cooperative Credit Society), more than 10 million members. Insurance, housing and fishery cooperatives are also strong, as well as health care and child care cooperatives. In the field of retail cooperatives a remarkable example is Mountain Equipment Co-op (MEC) established in 1971 by a small group of outdoor enthusiasts in Vancouver for the sale of outdoor equipment and apparel, which in 2006 had 2.3 million members and is leader in the use of internet technologies as well as in the running of sustainability and ethical programmes (Walzer and Merrett, 2000). Canada has also developed multi-stakeholder cooperatives and worker-shareholder cooperatives, formed after the rescuing of private enterprises by their employees. The two Canadian umbrella organizations – the French speaking Desjardins Group and the English speaking Canadian Cooperative Association born in 1909 (McPherson, 2009) – beside the services they render to their member cooperatives and second tier organizations, run programmes promoting cooperatives in the developing world. Today half of the Canadian population is a member of a cooperative, making Canada one of the most highly cooperative countries in the world.

4.9 JAPAN

When Japan opened up to the Western market economy in the nineteenth century, it did so across the board, and the cooperative movement spread from its beginning in the 1870s, patterned after European models. The first legislation regulating cooperatives was enacted in 1900, and under it the movement flourished, reaching a million members by 1912 and nearly 3 million members in 1922, belonging to 191 federations. The authoritarian governments that followed, like the European dictatorships, impeded the cooperative movement, but the post-war resurgence was dynamic indeed. Membership rose to 22 million in 1972 and 57 million two decades later. The strongest sectors are agriculture, consumer co-ops and insurance (with 14 million members). Farmers' cooperatives were the chosen instrument for applying government farm subsidies, performing a number of activities (supplying inputs, marketing of output, food processing, finance, insurance, building, and other rural services, including health and cultural services). So Japanese farmers' cooperatives became a power with over 10 million members and an enormous volume of business. In fact, they dominate Japanese agriculture, with a market share of 70 per cent at the end of the last century, and maintain social cohesion in the countryside. Today Japanese farmers' cooperatives must cope with the liberalization imposed by international agreements.

On the consumer front, the Japanese Consumer Cooperatives Union was formed in 1951 and began producing under its own brand in 1960. It now has a market share of 5 per cent and is the third largest retailer in a highly fragmented market. It has 572 co-ops with 22 million members who are still highly active in running their organizations. Half of the co-ops' total turnover depends on an original system of 'Han' groups that arrange for collective purchases and home delivery.

4.10 INDIA

In the developing world the country with the largest cooperative movement is certainly India, and not only because the country itself is so large. The movement originated in 1904 at the initiative of the British government, which enacted a law on cooperative credit societies that was extended to all cooperatives in 1912. In 1922 there were already over 50 000 co-ops in India, with 2 million members, and in 1929 the National Cooperative Union of India was formed, its member units present almost exclusively in the countryside. Among other things, cooperatives in India have been active in improving the conditions of lower castes members (Williams, 2007).

With independence and the separation of India and Pakistan, the first Indian governments embraced the idea of a thoroughly 'cooperativized' state, making the co-ops little more than an appendage to state economic planning. While certainly not encouraging autonomy and membership responsibility, imparting a top-down rather than a bottom-up orientation, this did greatly swell the number of organizations and their membership. There are now half a million cooperatives with 210 million members, organized into 214 federations under the central aegis of the umbrella organization NCUI. But it did not strengthen entrepreneurship, despite the presence of co-ops in all the rural villages and their large market shares: 37 per cent in fertilizer, 55 per cent in sugar, 50 per cent in animal feed, 60 per cent in cotton retailing, 51 per cent in cooking oils, 55 per cent in textiles, 62 per cent in rural storage facilities, 95 per cent in rubber, 46 per cent in rural credit, 28 per cent in wheat, 28 per cent in rural retail trade and a marginal presence in the cities.

The numbers make it clear that the Indian cooperative movement is vast and diversified, but restricted mostly to the countryside and subject to state direction. The law does not encourage capitalization of cooperatives, despite the legislative reform of 2002 enhancing democratic governance of the co-ops. The prospect now is for the expansion of the cooperative societies in size, the consolidation of the network of credit unions and the development of professional management to make cooperative enterprises competitive. This is a long-term objective.

More generally, it is worth underscoring that in the developing world cooperatives are an almost exclusively rural phenomenon, whereas in Western Europe, the USA and Canada they are also present in industry, in services and in the cities (Rajagopalan, 2007).

5. The cooperative movement in Italy

The Italian cooperative movement is not so well known abroad for a number of reasons, among which is the lack of effort to represent it in the English language, but it deserves attention for its long history and its capability to grow strongly in recent times, finding new paths. This is why we devote an entire chapter to its history.

5.1 THE ORIGINS

The origins of the cooperative movement in Italy date back to the first consumer co-op in Turin, founded in 1854, even though as in other countries there had been short-lived experiences earlier. In this case, as in most of the subsequent ones, the cultural and associative soil that delivered the first cooperatives consisted of the workers' mutual aid societies,[1] which began to be formed all over Europe in the later eighteenth century. These were the descendants of the old confraternities created by the guilds, which had been abolished by then. They took on a new form, maintaining their spirit of solidarity but organizing on a territorial rather than vocational basis and accompanying their traditional social insurance activities with new cultural and economic initiatives (Fornasari and Zamagni, 1997).

The mutual aid societies had a large membership base consisting of people of modest economic means but not destitute. Since these members could contribute their small savings to raise the initial capital, the societies were especially suitable for the creation of consumer, worker, credit and housing co-ops. And so the Italian cooperative movement began in the cities, not the countryside. And it began in particular in Piedmont, where many workers' associations had come into being even before the Albertine Statute, which formally guaranteed freedom of association in 1848.

---

[1]   In English they are better known as friendly societies.

The first worker cooperative in Italy was formed in 1856 in the town of Altare (in the Kingdom of Savoy), grouping glass workers. The first popular bank arose in Lodi in 1864 at the initiative of the local mutual aid society, but Italy adopted the limited form. It was followed by another one founded in Milan the next year and then by a wave of others; by 1880 there were 140 credit unions, all in limited form. Not until the farm crisis that swept Europe in the mid-1870s did things begin to happen in the countryside as well. The first farm labourers co-op was the General Association of Farm Labourers, formed in Ravenna in 1883 by Nullo Baldini. A decade later there were 525 such co-ops, 185 of them in the region of Emilia-Romagna. To cope with the lack of work in the countryside, the cooperatives would employ their members as construction workers as well, and so thus often became cooperatives of farm labourers and construction workers. The first rural credit union was founded by Leone Wollemborg in 1883 in Loreggia (near Padua). The first farmer supply cooperatives (agrarian consortia) appeared in the Po Valley in the 1880s, and in 1892 they formed a united federation headquartered in Piacenza. Now, thanks largely to the countless men and women who dedicated their lives to the cooperative movement – including Francesco Viganò, Luigi Luzzatti, Ugo Rabbeno, Nullo Baldini, Luigi Buffoli, Enea Cavalieri, Giovanni Raineri and Antonio Vergnanini, among many – Italian cooperation gained strength and, for the first time, official recognition in the Commercial Code enacted in 1882 (Book I, Title IX, Section VII was given over to cooperatives). The Commercial Code treated cooperative societies as on a par with the public limited company, but recognized their democratic governance on the principle of one person, one vote and the limits on members' shareholdings; the publication of cooperative societies' acts and documents was exempted from registration and stamp tax.

The first comprehensive statistics on Italian cooperative societies, released in 1890, found 1190 co-ops, not counting credit unions; of these 681 were consumer co-ops and 208 were social dairies. Eighty per cent were located in the north. The only non-northern region with a significant presence of co-ops was Tuscany, in the centre, which numbered 122 (10 per cent of the national total). Its role confirmed that the regional distribution of co-ops mirrored that of the older mutual societies. Not much information is available on the overall economic size of these cooperatives, but we do have detailed data on some of them with membership in the thousands and substantial sales, such as Unione Cooperativa, a consumer co-op formed in Milan in 1886, Unione

Militare in Rome (1890) and the Ravenna Farm Labourers Association itself, which specialized in land reclamation and carried out projects in Tuscany and near Rome as well.

For the most part the ideology of the earliest cooperatives was liberal, inspired by Mazzini, but in the 1880s socialist ideas began to spread and penetrate the cooperative movement. The representatives of 130 cooperative societies met in Milan in 1886, together with European cooperative leaders, including Holyoake, to found a Federation of Italian Cooperatives. At first the leadership belonged mainly to the original inspiration, although the gathering did approve a motion in support of 'movements for the organization and betterment of the working classes'. Gradually, however, the socialist presence strengthened. In 1893 the organization's name was changed to 'National Cooperative League of Italy,' and in 1898, at the tenth congress, came the rupture. A motion was presented to amend Article 3 of the League's statute as follows: 'The League is not concerned with politics or with religion. Cooperation is neutral ground. ... Every society belonging to the League recognizes that cooperation must not serve as the instrument of any party.' But the motion was not passed, and as a result the remaining non-socialist cooperatives left, including the Milan Unione Cooperativa. The League thus became a cooperative federation under Socialist Party hegemony. In 1899 it numbered 345 co-ops and had a membership of 227 000.

As the 1880s gave way to the 1890s, Catholics too began to become socially active. The key events were Giuseppe Toniolo's foundation of the Catholic Union for Social Studies in 1889 and the publication in 1891 of Pope Leo XIII's encyclical *Rerum Novarum*, setting the seal on the developments in social thought produced by Catholics in Italy, France, Belgium, Austria, Britain and Switzerland. In the economic area Catholics' efforts were concentrated in the proliferation of rural credit unions (which rose in number from 30 in 1892 to 779 in 1897) and farmer, dairy and winemaking co-ops, but they also constituted Catholic banks in the cities, although mainly in the form of limited companies, not cooperatives. In 1898 the Federation of Catholic Unions of Farmer Cooperatives was formed. The Catholic cooperative movement grew especially strong in Trentino under the leadership of Don Lorenzo Guetti, who created more than a hundred consumer co-ops (called 'cooperative families') and 60 rural credit unions between 1890 and 1898. The Federation of Cooperative Consortia, founded in Trento in 1895, is still in being today (Zaninelli, 1996).

5.2   THE FLOWERING OF COOPERATIVES BETWEEN THE GIOLITTI ERA AND WORLD WAR I

With the industrial take-off of northwestern Italy (the regions of Piedmont, Lombardy and Liguria) starting in 1896, which had some spillover effects in the rest of northern Italy as well, the cooperative movement also prospered, not least thanks to major legislation enacted by the government of Giovanni Giolitti. A number of laws concerning cooperatives were passed between 1904 and 1911, designed first to verify the genuinely cooperative nature of the societies eligible for public works contracts and then to permit their grouping in consortia in order to win larger contracts. On the occasion of the passage of the definitive regulations in 1911, the governance of worker cooperatives was redefined. The minimum membership was set at nine, the 'open door' principle was laid down, and greater discretion in deciding the distribution of profits was allowed. Further, the police prefectures' powers of control over the cooperatives listed in the official registers established in 1890 were confirmed.

Soon a good many consortia formed, chiefly in Emilia-Romagna, Lombardy, Veneto and Rome, and the volume of the cooperatives' public works contracting increased. Because Emilia-Romagna was very active in the formation of farm labourer and construction worker cooperatives and consortia, by the eve of World War I that region had actually taken a narrow lead over Lombardy in total number of co-ops. Previously, when consumer co-ops were the prevalent form, Lombardy had held the numerical edge (in fact, in 1913 there were 636 consumer co-ops there compared with 325 in Emilia-Romagna).

There was an effort to upgrade the consumer co-ops as well, given their large numbers (one-third of all Italian co-ops, excluding credit unions, at the outbreak of the war) and the presence of some major organizations, such as the Turin Cooperative Alliance (ACT), Unione Cooperativa in Milan, the Cooperative Operaie (workers' cooperatives) in Trieste and Unione Militare in Rome. For years the question of forming wholesale consortia, patterned after the British wholesale cooperatives, had been on the agenda. But the fragmentation and territorial dispersion of Italian co-ops made it hard to find suitable locations for warehouses. The result was the formation of local consortia with small warehouses, whose efforts at national coordination failed repeatedly.

Finally, in 1911, on the basis of one local consortium that was more solid than the rest, the 'Italian Consortium of Consumer Cooperatives' came into being. Success did not smile upon this initiative either, however, and by the end of 1912 just 150 of Italy's 2500 consumer co-ops had joined. Decades would pass before this difficulty for consumer cooperatives could be resolved.

Popular banks flourished. In 1910 they numbered 850, with half a million members and a market share equal to nearly a fourth of all bank assets (not counting the banks of issue and the postal Deposits and Loans Fund). So did rural credit unions, mainly Catholic, which by the war numbered over 2500 and had some 200 000 members; many of these, however, were informal bodies not included in the statistics of the Bank of Italy (which counted only half of them), with a total volume of business of no more than 2 per cent of banking system assets. Where cooperative banks were spread throughout the national territory, with a significant presence in the south, the rural credit unions were found mostly in the north, but with a presence in Sicily as well, where Don Luigi Sturzo championed them. In 1904 the Humanitarian Society in Milan sponsored the formation of the Institute for Cooperative Credit, which quickly spawned an interregional network of agencies, also taking over the Banca di Reggio Emilia. On the strength of this example, the main advocate of cooperative credit in Italy, Luigi Luzzatti, succeeded in creating a national organization. On 9 June 1913 the National Institute for Cooperative Credit was formed in Rome, with the substantial participation of savings banks as well as the Bank of Italy and the national retirement fund.

Meanwhile, the divide between the 'red' cooperatives of the League and the 'white' ones organized by the Catholics deepened. By now the Catholic cooperative movement too had organized into territorial and sectoral federations, but it was not until the end of World War I that it constituted a national body. The old liberal cooperatives remained fragmented, not a part of either of the two large umbrella organizations. The only significant organization within this strand of the movement was the Autonomous Consortium of Cooperatives of the Province of Ravenna, founded in 1910 by Pietro Bondi, which brought together 50 co-ops united by republican ideas.

The war saw the multiplication of cooperatives, for a number of reasons. Government rationing made broad use of the consumer co-ops to prevent speculation and black marketeering. Upstream, consumer agencies were constituted as suppliers; by the end of the conflict they numbered 250. At the same time, worker cooperatives strengthened thanks to war and state supply contracts, and the farmer co-ops also prospered, because they were asked to provide labour (often enough female labour) in the place of the peasants sent to the front. The time, then, was ripe for a further step forward in organization. In 1917 the League formed national federations (consumer cooperatives, headquartered in Milan; worker cooperatives, in Rome; farmer cooperatives, in Bologna). The Catholic movement created a national federation of consumer cooperatives in 1917 to flank its Federation of Rural Credit Unions and Catholic Union of Farmer Cooperatives. In September 1918 this wing of the movement founded the Italian Cooperative Confederation. The organizing committee held its first meeting on 14 May 1919 – considered the foundation date – and the first congress was held in Treviso in April 1921, grouping 7365 societies, including 3200 consumer co-ops and 2166 rural credit unions. In an interview on the occasion of the first congress, the ICC general secretary Ercole Chiri called cooperation 'a form of activity that is independent and susceptible to unlimited development; it is its own *raison d'être*, in that it emancipates the popular masses from all suffocating hegemony'. By 1921 there were some 20 000 cooperatives in Italy (not counting the cooperative banks), of which some 40 per cent were worker co-ops (Zangheri, 1987).

5.3 THE ATTACK OF FASCISM AND SURVIVAL IN THE FASCIST REGIME

The downturn started in 1922. First of all, a price decline after years of inflation weakened a good many co-ops, especially farmer and consumer co-ops, which had more trouble adapting. There were severe repercussions for the National Institute for Cooperative Credit. More important was a violent press campaign against cooperatives, accompanied by physical assaults on co-op premises and members by the fascist veterans' groups founded by Mussolini in 1919. The attacks focused mainly on the 'red' cooperatives, but the others did not escape either, such as the glorious ACT alliance in Turin, descendant of Italy's first consumer co-op. The attacks on ACT, which had a good many branches, were devastating, and its governing board elected to turn the entire organization over to the prefect of police. In 1923 the latter designated it as a foundation with a president named by the prefect himself (the

Cooperative Operaie, or 'workers' cooperatives', of Trieste would share this fate in 1935). After this campaign of destruction, the fascists sought to take over the presidency of the federations and of single co-ops. This was the case with the Cooperative Union of Milan, which had 107 stores and 110 million lire in sales in 1921; it was the largest consumer co-op, followed by ACT with 78 million lire and the Cooperative Operaie with 71 million. In 1923 the special commissioner (fascist) named by the prefect liquidated the bulk of the Union's assets and cut its outlets and sales in half, throwing it into an irreversible decline that ended within a few years in its winding up. The National Institute for Cooperative Credit, in serious trouble since 1922, was also acquired by the fascists, who reformed it by decree in 1923 and then turned it into an institution to finance the fascist regime's public works projects under the name *'Banca nazionale del lavoro e della cooperazione'* in 1927.[2]

In 1925 Parliament was abolished and the corporative transformation of the state began in earnest. What was left of the cooperative movement was consolidated under a single representative body, founded in 1926 as the National Fascist Cooperative Agency responsible for assistance, development and coordination of cooperatives (except mutual credit unions). This ushered in a very dark time for the movement, which was obliged to fit into a top-down, state planned and corporatist order that ran counter to its ideals of economic and administrative democracy.

Nevertheless, it is wrong to maintain that the survival of many co-ops and even the creation of some new ones are not worth writing about. For the fact is that not even fascism managed to crush the cooperative movement in Italy, which indeed, as we shall see, subsequently recovered with great strength. Put another way, the impact of the fascist dictatorship on cooperatives was not as devastating as in Spain or Germany, partly because the National Fascist Cooperative Agency did in fact consolidate the co-ops and the fascist regime continued to award public works contracts to them and partly because in many cases their middle-level technicians and managers, and even some top managers, remained in their positions and so were able to preserve the values of the movement.

The cooperatives that gained most notably under fascism were food

---

2   In 1929 the name was shortened to just *Banca nazionale del lavoro* (National Labour Bank).

processing co-ops, while the supply cooperatives (agrarian consortia) were removed from the cooperative sphere and made over into quasi-governmental agencies that among other things were responsible for running the regime's compulsory stockpiling programme for farm commodities in the 1930s. Building cooperatives were assigned public works contracts and the construction of very low-cost housing, designed to attenuate the job losses provoked by the crash of 1929.

Consumer cooperatives, though still relatively prosperous as the 1920s drew to a close – 3334 societies with 825 000 members – were hard hit by the Depression (as were major retailers in general). The fascist regime sought to shore the sector up, reviving the idea of the cooperative wholesale warehouse and founding, in 1927, the Central Supply Agency, which in 1938 became the Italian Cooperative Supply Agency. But the agency never managed to play a truly important role. At the end of the 1930s consumer co-ops numbered 2893, with a membership of 600 000. Mutual credit societies declined even more sharply, partly because the fascist banking laws required greater organizational formalities, prompting a series of mergers, and partly because of the 1929 crash and its aftermath. The 1930s ended with a thousand mutual 'rural and artisans' banks' (this name was adopted in 1938) and 267 popular banks.

Finally, in the 1942 Commercial Code, Title VI, Book V, Articles 2511–2544, for the first time the regime distinguished cooperatives from other enterprises on the basis of their purpose of mutual aid, leaving open its definition.

5.4   POST-WAR REVIVAL AND REORGANIZATION

At the fall of the fascist regime, the Italian cooperative movement consisted of an estimated 12 000 co-ops with 3 million members. In 1944 the leaders of the movement launched a campaign to keep the National Fascist Cooperative Agency in being (under another name, obviously) as a unitary, democratic, apolitical body embracing all the cooperatives. But the time was not yet ripe to transcend ideological divisions. The Italian Cooperative Confederation, the Catholic umbrella organization, was reconstituted on 5 May 1945 (in 1967 it would become the Italian Confederation of Cooperatives, 'Confcooperative'), and on 3 September the National League of Cooperatives and Mutual Societies (in 1996 it became Legacoop). At first the League grouped all the non-Catholic co-ops, but it was soon dominated by the Communist current.[3]

These ideological divisions did not prevent a united effort to include explicit mention of cooperation in the new Republican Constitution (1948), in Article 45, which reads:

> The Republic recognizes the *social* function of mutual cooperation, with no private speculative aim. The law shall promote and foster its growth by the most suitable means and shall guarantee its nature and purposes *with special controls*. (emphasis added).

Thus two conditions must be fulfilled in order to gain recognition as a cooperative: mutual aid and absence of speculative motive. The Basevi[4] Law of 14 December 1947 defined the criteria for the two conditions: an open door and one person, one vote, but also a ban on members' ownership of businesses in the same or related fields as the cooperative, a ban on dividends exceeding the 'legal rate of interest', a ban on the distribution of indivisible reserves to members, and in the case of winding up the remaining assets to be devolved to activities in the public interest. The supervision of cooperatives was entrusted to the cooperative umbrella organizations for their members and to the Labor Ministry for co-ops not belonging to any such organization. Cooperatives interested in the special benefits of the law (tax allowances) had to be entered in a special register kept by the prefect. As many legal scholars have observed, these criteria mean that the members are not the owners of the cooperative enterprise as individuals. Rather, they can use this collective, intergenerational ownership for mutual aid. In other words, they administer assets that are not fully at their disposal. This is precisely the element – serving a general interest – that justifies public control of the cooperative, as Article 45 specifies.

Also, two most important consequences of this Italian legislation on cooperatives need highlighting. First was the political and cultural compromise of the twentieth century, which heavily affected legislation. The essence of this compromise is that the state does offer economic

---

3   The other two of today's umbrella cooperative organizations were created later: the General Association of Italian Cooperatives (Agci) in 1952, founded by Republicans and Social Democrats who had left the League, and the National Union of Italian Cooperative (Unci), formed in 1975 by a split from the Catholic Confederation.

4   Alberto Basevi was a well known leader of the Italian cooperative movement and the parliamentary sponsor of the bill.

incentives to cooperative enterprises in the form of tax allowances, but on condition that they accept a niche role with respect to capitalistic and state-owned corporations. The aim – unavowed but readily perceptible in any number of statements and documents – is to make sure that co-ops do not get in the way of the other forms of enterprise, on which national economic development was assumed to depend.

This may help explain why the Italian cooperative movement has long suffered from what psychologists call the 'Peter Pan' syndrome: the idea that the cooperative identity can be preserved only on a small scale, in the interstices of the market. It was not until the 1997 Pandolfi Bill (see below) that things began to change, and people began to see that the co-op is actually just a different way of doing business, an original way of interpreting economic action that does not separate but actually brings together the social and the economic aspects. In fact, maintaining that the cooperative identity is best preserved by staying small in size would be like arguing that no large State can be truly democratic, because the methods of the Greek *polis* are not practicable. But the opposite is true: the larger the cooperative, the stronger its identity and the greater its capacity to infect the rest of the market. If a co-op were to choose to remain stationary, not to grow, it would fall into a blatant pragmatic contradiction (although there is no denying that expansion does raise serious problems of identity). There are no economies or diseconomies of scale specific to the form of enterprise, so the assertion that a cooperative, as such, cannot aspire to large size is unfounded. Instead, it is the historical conditions of the market and productive technology that determine whether a firm should be large or small. Certainly, its legal or institutional form cannot lay down a rule of conduct.

Among later measures, certainly the most significant were those producing capital strengthening: the series of laws beginning in 1971 that favoured members' direct loans to co-ops, an instrument used chiefly by consumer cooperatives; Law 904/1977 (named after the minister Pandolfi), instituting tax exemption for earnings retained as indivisible reserves (that is, capital that cannot be distributed to members); a 1983 law (named after the minister Visentini), explicitly reaffirming that cooperatives may constitute, purchase or have holdings in joint stock companies and partnerships; Law 381/1991, introducing special legislation for social cooperatives; Law 59/1992 further extending the possibilities of funding by introducing the figure of the member investor and the cooperative participation shares (a sort of preference share) as well as the so-called promotion fund, financed by 3 per cent of the member co-ops' profits and managed by the umbrella organizations with the aim of consolidating and enlarging the movement (Bulgarelli and Viviani, 2006).

Finally, the Berlusconi government's overall company law reform designed by Law 366/2001 and implemented by a Legislative Decree in 2003 was vehemently criticized by the cooperatives, which for the first time were not favoured. The dispute turned on the definition of cooperatives and on the tax benefits. It ended with a distinction between constitutional co-ops (acting predominantly for members) and others,[5] and a limit to the amount of profits that could be allocated to indivisible reserves with tax exemption. The law also made possible the conversion of cooperatives into capitalist firms, though the assets accumulated as indivisible reserves still had to be earmarked for social purposes.

The official sources for an overview of cooperative enterprises since World War II in Italy are unsatisfactory. Various studies have sought to plug the holes in our knowledge. The census data from the National Statistical Institute (Istat) certainly underestimate the size of the cooperative sector up until 1971. As Table 5.1 shows, Istat documents the slow growth of cooperation until that year and its rapid growth thereafter, with a surge in the 1990s, when the rest of the economy slowed down. Employment growth in cooperatives was 60.1 per cent during that decade, compared with 9.1 per cent overall. Cooperatives thus

Table 5.1   Cooperative enterprises in the census, 1951–2001

	No. of co-ops	% of all enterprises*	No. of workers	% of all workers*
1951	10 782	0.7	137 885	2.0
1961	12 229	0.6	192 008	2.2
1971	10 744	0.5	207 477	1.9
1981	19 900	0.7	362 435	2.8
1991	35 646	1.1	584 322	4.0
2001	53 393	1.2	935 239	5.8

Note: * Excluding public administration.

Source: Istat, *Censimenti dell'industria e dei servizi*, (various years).

---

5   Over nine-tenths of the co-ops qualified in the former category.

Table 5.2 Cooperative workers by economic sector

	1971	1981	1991	2001
Agriculture and fisheries	32 660	33 795	27 948	36 917
Manufacturing	44 213	90 355	112 762	85 815
Construction	32 168	58 811	61 654	57 796
Wholesale & retail trade	25 386	44 078	83 611	74 047
Other services	73 050	135 396	270 837	531 517
Social co-ops			27 510	149 147
Total	207 477	362 435	584 322	935 239

Source: Istat, *Censimenti dell'industria e dei servizi* (various years).

accounted for a quarter of all the jobs created between 1991 and 2001. The number of workers in social cooperatives rose nearly sixfold, from 27 510 to 149 147; and it continued to increase thereafter.

Censuses also show the growing size of the cooperatives. The share of workers accounted for by cooperatives has risen faster in the larger enterprises than overall. In 2001 cooperatives accounted for 5 per cent

Table 5.3 Cooperative workforce by region

	Cooperatives excluding social co-ops			Social co-ops 2001
	% 1971	% 2001	% increase 2001/1971	
Northwest local units	23.5	27.0	3.4	31.7
Northeast local units	39.8	31.0	1.9	28.3
Emilia-Romagna local units	*25.1*	*16.9*	*1.6*	
Centre local units	16.7	19.9	3.5	20.7
Tuscany local units	*8.5*	*6.7*	*2.0*	
Mainland South local units	13.0	15.1	3.4	10.0
Island regions local units	7.0	7.0	2.8	9.3
Total	100	100	2.8	100

Source: Istat, *Censimenti dell'industria e dei servizi* (various years).

of total employment in industry and services (excluding social co-ops); but in enterprises with 50 or more workers, they accounted for 9.3 per cent of employment. This discovery of the progressive flowering of co-ops among large Italian enterprises suggests that the cooperative movement should be considered as an emerging force in Italian business. But before undertaking such an analysis, let us examine the Istat data more closely, breaking them down by sector and region (Tables 5.2 and 5.3). This leads to two main conclusions.

1. By sector, as Italian cooperation developed in the post-war period, there was a very substantial relative gain for the services. The traditional domination of farming and related activities gave way to the various services: credit, insurance, trade (consumption), transport and miscellaneous, including restaurants and the like, cleaning and maintenance, and social services. The attempt to gain a position in industry produced rare if significant successes in manufacturing (outside of food and beverages) and quite substantial success in construction (with links to housing cooperatives). So some sectors in particular are favoured by the cooperative movement, with a much larger than average incidence on total sectoral employment. These sectors of the economy, where cooperatives have clearly approached 'critical mass', will be the object of more detailed treatment later.

2. Geographically, the regions most favoured by the movement are Emilia-Romagna, Trentino and Tuscany, but some others have also developed strongly. In 2001 the leadership remained firmly in the hands of one of the historical cradles of the movement, Emilia-Romagna, which accounted for 9.8 per cent of all non-farm cooperative workers. However, Table 5.3 shows that between 1971 and 2001 growth was faster outside the traditional centres of cooperation, due in part to the expansion of established cooperatives in new parts of the country.

The recent consolidation of cooperative enterprises in Italy suggests the need for further refinement of the survey on large firms (those with 500 workers or more). In this size class, cooperatives gained ground rapidly between 1971 and 2001, as Table 5.4 indicates. The number of these enterprises increased throughout the period, their size above all in the last decade, and in just a few sectors. By number, from 2.3 per cent of large Italian firms in 1971, the co-ops rose to 9 per cent in 2001; and

*Table 5. 4   Cooperative enterprises with 500 or more workers**

	No. of enterprises				No. of workers			
	1971	1981	1991	2001	1971	1981	1991	2001
Agriculture	1	3	0	0	2 166	3 815	0	0
Fisheries	2	0	0	0	1 063	0	0	0
Manufacturing	3	7	13	13	1 980	5 065	13 476	16 522
of which food processing	*3*	*7*	*8*	*10*	*1 980*	*5 065*	*6 193*	*13 429*
Construction	3	17	15	7	3 344	15 690	12 269	5 943
Trade	5	11	15	16	2 899	9 000	21 804	35 095
Hotels, restaurants	0	2	3	5	0	1 528	3 986	15 555
Transport, etc.	8	4	1	17	14 231	2 984	553	11 569
Financial intermediation	6	12	30	24	9 518	21 270	40 707	55 584
Facility management services	0	2	11	34	0	1 468	11 709	57 477
of which cleaning	*0*	*1*	*9*	*32*	*0*	*1 468*	*9 776*	*47 150*
Health and other services	0	0	0	3	0	0	0	3 329
Other social services	0	0	1	2	0	0	1 019	1 685
Total	28	58	89	121	35 201	60 820	105 523	202 759
Workers per cooperative					1 257	1 049	1 186	1 676

Note: * Excluding social cooperatives.

Source: Istat, *Censimenti dell'industria e dei servizi* (various years).

Table 5.5   Large Italian cooperatives (500 workers or more) in 2004

	Number of cooperatives	Sales (millions of euros)	Number of workers	Member- ship[a]
Manufacturing	20	6 738	27 453	75 480
Food & beverages	(17)	(5 201)	(20 606)	(75 000)
Construction	15	5 189	16 661	8 000
Retail chains	27	23 807	94 128	5 514 404
COOP	(11)	(11 011)	(49 394)	(5 507 000)
CONAD	(9)	(6 300)	(26 259)	(3 527)
Other	(7)	(6 496)	(18 475)	(3 877)
Other services	43	3 453	120 024	826 072
Facility management	(27)	(1 973)	(55 913)	(18 605)
Restaurant hotel	(4)	(1 082)	(21 849)	(20 806)
Logistics	(5)	(159)	(3 712)	(2 010)
Other	(4)	(239)	(2 450)	(10 427)
Finance[b]	(3)	–	(36 100)	(774 224)
Total	105	39 187	258 266	6 423 956

Notes:
[a] In some cases members are enterprises or second-level cooperatives, so the total number is only indicative.
[b] Two insurance companies, of which one (Unipol) is Italy's third-largest, plus the entire system of mutual banks, consisting of 440 banks with 3499 branches (11.2 per cent of the national total), and fund raising equal to 8.4 per cent of the total.

Source: Financial statements of co-ops belonging to Legacoop, plus some members of Confcooperative.

by workforce, from 1.2 per cent to 8.1 per cent. That is, the cooperatives moved against the overall trend in the Italian economy: where the average size of capitalist firms tended to diminish, that of the cooperatives increased.

In 2001 in the food processing industry cooperatives accounted for 18.2 per cent of all workers in firms with over 500 workers; in construction 22.8 per cent; in trade 15.7 per cent; in hotels and restaurants 19.3 per cent; in financial intermediation 16.5 per cent; in facility management services services 17.3 per cent (including 42.7 per cent in cleaning services), and in health and social services (excluding social co-ops) 22.2 per cent. Large cooperative enterprises have vanished only in agri-

Table 5.6   The Italian cooperative movement in 2006

	Number of enterprises	Sales (billions of euros)	Members	Direct employees
Legacoop	15 200	50	7 500 000	414 000
Confcooperative	19 200	57	2 878 000	466 000
AGCI	5 768	6	439 000	70 000[a]
UNCI	7 825	3[a]	558 000	129 000
Unicoop[c]	1 910	0.3[a]	15 000	20 000[a]
Not belonging to the above	21 561[b]	3[a]	100 000[a]	150 000[a]
Total	71 464	119	11 490 000	1 249 000

Notes:
[a]   Estimated.
[b]   Estimated as a residual, with respect to the total of 71 464 according to Chamber of Commerce data in Unioncamere, *Secondo rapporto sulle imprese cooperative* (2006). Note that the number of co-ops entered in the register instituted on 15 January 2006 was 62 253, indicating that the earlier figures were overestimated because they included inactive cooperatives, most of which are classed among those not belonging to any umbrella organization (bringing that figure down to about 12 000 in realistic terms).
[c]   A fifth umbrella organization was recognized on 7 May 2004.

Source: Based on official data from the central cooperative organizations.

culture and fishing, following the national trend. More details on some of the largest co-ops can be found in Table 5.5.

To properly appreciate the importance of Italian cooperative enterprises today, look at Table 5.6 which provides data for 2006. The two leading umbrella organizations, Legacoop and Confcooperative, are equivalent in size. Their composition differs considerably, however, as Legacoop has more large cooperatives and groups. A comparison with the 105 large cooperatives shown in Table 5.5 reveals that these represent just 0.15 to 0.17 per cent of all Italian co-ops (depending on which total one uses) but 57.6 per cent of membership, 34 per cent of turnover and 21.7 per cent of the workforce.

There were essentially two waves in the rise of Italian cooperatives from marginal to major status. The first, in the 1970s and early 1980s, saw the operational and management consolidation of individual co-ops, with expansion through mergers and the formation of networks (consortiums, for the most part) in geographically limited areas. The second wave, after a pause, came in the 1990s, with the formation of tighter cooperative networks (Menzani and Zamagni, 2009), including the formation of groups, amplifying an existing tendency to the creation (or acquisition) of non-cooperative enterprises controlled by co-ops. In some sectors large cooperatives were instrumental in aggregating and coordinating small and medium-sized enterprises (co-ops and others) in their areas, in part through the explicit formation of groups but also in part through related economic activities, and the revival of consortia at the national level.

We shall now briefly look at the economic sectors in which cooperatives are strongest.

5.5   WHOLESALE AND RETAIL TRADE

The cooperative movement is the Italian leader in large-scale distribution. Today two Legacoop organizations are active in this sector. One is ANCC, which groups 140 consumer co-ops under the Coop brand (the top nine account for 90 per cent of total sales) and has a powerful wholesale structure, Coop Italia, that has also brought together other groups of consumer and retailer cooperatives (Sait, Sigman, Despar) plus some small non-cooperative supermarket chains, with the foundation of Centrale Italiana. Total sales account for a quarter of Italian large-scale retailing turnover (Zamagni et al., 2004). The second Legacoop organization is ANCD, which groups consortiums of retailer cooperatives (CONAD and some minor brands), with 3000 outlets and sales volume equal to 12 per cent of total chain retail turnover. In February 2006 CONAD joined with the Belgian chain Coruyt (third-largest in that country), the Swiss Coop chain (number two), the Leclerc group in France (that country's top hypermarket chain) and Rewe (Germany's number two chain) to constitute Copernic, the first European-law cooperative, with total sales of 96 billion and 17 500 sales outlets. Overall, then, Legacoop accounts for more than a third of large-scale retail outlet turnover in Italy, and the share is rising.

The key to this remarkable success can be traced back to the 1970s. In the face of crisis at a number of cooperative enterprises and the severe operating problems caused by rapid inflation, some of Italy's leading co-ops reacted decisively, speeding up the modernization of their supermarket outlets by a series of mergers and taking a more professional approach to the market, concentrating on a single brand – Coop – and greatly stepping up advertising. Naturally, some of the preconditions for this advance had already been put in place, such as the creation of Coop Italia back in 1967 and the area consortia (Battilani, 1999). But it was only in the 1970s that the tendency to favour mergers snowballed, and not until the end of that decade did turnover begin to rise rapidly. In 1983 there were still some 600 consumer co-ops; ten years later they numbered just 300, and the top nine made 78 per cent of all their sales. The second key move came in the 1990s, with the general shift to hypermarkets (Coop alone increased its hypermarket network from five in 1988 to 67 in 2003), and sales soared for both Coop and CONAD.

5.6   CONSTRUCTION

Italy's building industry is populated by myriads of tiny, even individual, firms; the overall average is just 2.5 workers per firm. The cooperative sector, in contrast, has succeeded in greatly strengthening single co-ops (a score have grown into large enterprises, and some, such as CMC and ACMAR, both of Ravenna, the latter belonging to the AGCI central organization, are among Italy's leading construction firms). Above all, it has formed major local consortiums and built them, eventually, into a national consortium. The local groupings arose as far back as the start of the twentieth century, but the decisive step towards a nationwide consortium did not come until 1978, with the merger of the powerful groups in Bologna (formed in 1912), Modena (1914) and Ferrara (1945) to form the Consortium of Construction Cooperatives (Consorzio Cooperative Costruzioni, CCC). Following this amalgamation, the CCC became increasingly important in promoting activities and providing services, and its operations more and more stretched beyond its home regions. At this point the idea was to unify all the consortia found in other regions under the CCC (by far the largest) to create a national consortium for overall strategic coordination of Legacoop's construction activity. This was finally achieved in 1990 (Fabbri, 1994). The last step was the takeover of the national cooperative supply consortium (Consorzio nazionale cooperative approvvigionamenti), ACAM. This grouped co-ops providing services for construction enterprises. The CCC now numbers 230 member co-ops and some 20 000 workers. With a turnover of 5 billion euros in 2008, it is the leading construction group in Italy and counts on a number of large enterprises, like the CMC, Ravenna (with sales of 640 million euros in 2006).

5.7   FOOD PROCESSING

Coordination of the co-ops engaged in food processing was more difficult. Enterprises regularly expanded by mergers, and now cooperative groups specialized according to product line are beginning to emerge. The largest, belonging to both Legacoop and Confcooperative, is in the dairy industry: the Granlatte-Granarolo group (Bertagnoni, 2004), with sales of 1 billion euros in 2008. Legacoop has also formed other large groups: producers of *grana padano* cheese (Granterre); wine (Cantine cooperative riunite and GIV); truck farming (Apofruit Italia); extensive crops, products and services (Progeo); and meats (Unipeg). Confcooperative also has a substantial presence in the food processing sector, with such major groups as the cannery chain Consorzio Conserve Italia (1 billion euros of turnover in 2008), which was formed in 1976 and has been operational since 1978. It has internationalized with the acquisition of French, German, Polish and Spanish enterprises and has strengthened itself with numerous acquisitions in Italy as well, including that of Cirio-De Rica in 2004. In 1967, Confcooperative had also created Consorzio Emiliano dell'ortofrutta (now APO-Conerpo). In winemaking, the Caviro consortium, founded in 1966, is Italy's leading distributor of wines packaged in carton packs and also the country's leading producer of concentrated must and alcohol distilled from wine.

We lack an overall study of the presence of the cooperative movement in the food processing sector (Zuppiroli and Vecchio, 2006), but there is no doubt that cooperatives are at the forefront in Italy's effort to capitalize on its typical export products and on its special Mediterranean diet, remaining competitive vis-à-vis the multinational food giants (as in the retailing industry).

5.8   FACILITY MANAGEMENT AND OTHER SERVICES

More recently, Italian cooperatives have organized groups in the service sector as well. The largest is Manutencoop, specializing in facility management services, with a turnover of over 700 million euros in 2008. Created in the 1930s in Bologna as a cooperative for railroad cleaning, Manutencoop is now a nationwide colossus with divisions specializing in hospital cleaning, general maintenance for large facilities and waste treatment. Four other cooperatives are among the ten leading Italian firms in the sector: Coopservice di Reggio Emilia, Teamservice, La

Fiorita and Coop Lat. There are now two national consortiums, increasingly able to provide customers with full service packages by combining the expertise of several different co-ops. Ciclat, formed in Bologna in 1953 but in full-scale operation only since the 1970s, a member of Confcooperative, now groups a hundred or more co-ops active in maintenance, waste collection, restaurant services, shipping and security. CNS, belonging to Legacoop, was founded in Bologna in 1977 and began to function effectively in the later 1980s (Battilani and Bertagnoni, 2007). It now groups over 200 co-ops in facility management, transportation, porterage, custodianship and cleaning, ecology, restaurants and also tourist and cultural services. CNS as such has a turnover of some 500 million euros (2008), while that of its member cooperatives is considerably greater, because the biggest still operate largely on their own, outside the group. Another noteworthy organization is the CAMST restaurant and catering cooperative (Zamagni, 2002), created in 1945 originally to operate the Bologna railway station buffet service, then other such services, then canteens and food services for firms, hospitals and schools, then catering. CAMST is now very widespread in northern Italy and is big enough (over 800 million euros of turnover) to rival the main multinational firms (mostly French) active in Italy in restaurant services.

5.9   SOCIAL SERVICES

Social service co-ops have proliferated, notably because local government has tended to go over to outsourcing. The law now distinguishes between two types of co-ops. 'Type A' social service co-ops (accounting for two-thirds of total turnover) provide social and health care, educational, sporting and recreational services, especially to the socially disadvantaged, by operating residences, shelters and day care facilities, communities and day facilities and by offering at-home services. 'Type B' social service co-ops have the purpose of work integration for the disadvantaged and people in difficulty. In 2003 Italy had 6000 social co-ops with 220 000 workers, not counting volunteers. Confcooperative includes the extremely powerful consortium of social cooperatives CGM, created in 1987 and in 2008 grouping 75 local consortia embracing 1350 co-ops with 35 000 workers and a business volume of 1 billion euros. Legacoop also comprises a large number of social co-ops (1500, with 55 000 workers and 1.8 billion euros in turnover in 2008) and has formed a national association (Legacoopsociali), but its consortia are still small, although some, notably the one formed by the Cadiai cooperative enterprise, are growing rapidly.

Social cooperatives have played a decisive role in the reform of the Italian welfare system. The transition – still just beginning – from the obsolete model of welfare aiming to improve beneficiaries' living conditions to one designed to enhance their capabilities would have been inconceivable without the unexpected positive results of the social co-ops. Law 328/2000 – explicitly instituting horizontal subsidiarity as the standard in the new welfare system – is itself indebted to the multiple experiences of the social cooperatives (Borzaga and Ianes, 2006).

5.10   MUTUAL CREDIT AND INSURANCE

The 'rural and artisans banks' (credit unions), which were already organized on a regional basis, constituted a nationwide federation (Federcasse) in 1950 (Cafaro, 2001). In 1967 this organization joined Confcooperative. A period of rapid growth began in the 1960s. In 1963 ICCREA, a central credit institute for these rural and artisans banks, was founded to serve as a clearing house and provide assistance and specialized intermediation. With the banking reform of 1993 the banks took on the new name of 'cooperative credit banks' and were allowed to extend their range of business both in terms of services and in terms of territory. The last ten years have brought considerable strengthening. Cooperative credit unions now number 438 with 800 000 members and 30 000 employees. They are present in 2450 municipalities, especially the smaller ones, and account in 2008 for 9 per cent of total Italian bank deposits.

Another wing of cooperative credit in Italy is constituted by the cooperative banks termed popular banks, which before World War II were an integral part of the cooperative movement. Law 105/1948 recognized their democratic ownership and governance arrangements (one person, one vote and strict limits on shareholding), but they were not covered by the special legislation on cooperatives, so that they remained outside the grasp of umbrella organizations. In the past 30 years they have grown enormously, and in 2002 they had a banking market share of 17 per cent, but their cooperative identity has been seriously watered down, owing largely to a series of mergers with non-cooperative banks. Today they are struggling to find a new configuration – some would like it to be more cooperative, others more capitalistic. One new entry worth mentioning is Banca Etica (the ethical bank), constituted in 1998 by a group of non-profit associations to finance projects for social development and solidarity. Banca Etica has renewed the solidaristic roots of the cooperative banks.

Finally, the cooperative movement also has a massive presence in the insurance industry, counting a good number of mutual insurance societies, such as Società Cattolica di Assicurazioni in Verona (founded in 1896), and above all Unipol. Unipol was founded in the early 1960s when a large group of cooperatives in and near Bologna intended to constitute a cooperative insurance company but the necessary government authorization was too slow in coming. Instead, they took over a public limited insurance company that had been formed by Lancia in 1961 but had never started operations. And so in 1963, 230 cooperatives of Legacoop in Emilia-Romagna bought the Unipol insurance company. After a slow start, the company grew significantly in the 1970s and 1980s. In 1986 it obtained stock exchange listing, and thereafter expanded with various corporate takeovers to become the third or fourth largest Italian insurance company. Unipol was in the headlines in 2005 for its unsuccessful takeover bid for Banca nazionale del lavoro, which resulted in judicial proceedings (see Zamagni and Felice, 2006). The case is emblematic of the severe problems of governance of large cooperative groups, which will be treated specifically in Chapter 7.

6. The economic performance of cooperative enterprises

6.1 THE NEOCLASSICAL APPROACH

Now that we are familiar with the history and the identity of the cooperative enterprise, the question is whether it can truly compete with the capitalist firm in the marketplace. Answering this question means trying to determine the strengths and weaknesses of the two forms of enterprise. Virtually the entire literature devoted to such a comparison over the past half-century has taken as the gauge of their relative performance the standard one of 'efficiency'. Obviously this choice is precisely grounded. If in the long run in a market economy only efficient enterprises can survive the process of selection, then determining which form is more efficient is tantamount to determining the factors that predict the long-run success of one or the other.

How is this methodological choice translated into practice? The first point is that an enterprise is a coalition of persons supplying the inputs needed for a given production process, whose output is sold in the market. Since the relationships between these persons and the enterprise itself are governed by inherently incomplete contracts, it follows that some of them must be assigned the task of overseeing production activity. Let us assume, for simplicity, that the only ones who can perform this task are the suppliers of capital and the suppliers of labour (for the sake of brevity the others, such as the suppliers of raw materials or consumers, are left out, but the logic of the argument is in no way affected). Whichever economic agent is charged to control the enterprise, the fact is that the attribution of authority always, implicitly, entails the risk of abuse. The person with the ultimate power to check and control can impose costs or diminish benefits for the other members of the group, who in turn can do little indeed to alleviate the consequences. Basically, the reason is that within the enterprise – unlike the market – on-the-spot negotiations between controller and those controlled are not possible. Only in extreme cases, or in the event of grave abuses of power, will the members subjected to the abuse of power threaten to use the 'exit' option. On this basis we can seek out the factors that explain the differing ability of the suppliers of capital and of labour to exercise the ultimate power of control. The type of enterprise that emerges victorious in this match-up, and that will therefore ultimately prevail in the market, is the one that is most efficient in exercising control.

Let us examine the main results of the economic literature in this regard in recent decades. As mentioned earlier, the first significant contribution was that of the American economist Benjamin Ward (1958), who ascribed the differing performance of cooperative and capitalist enterprises to their different objective functions. His model made two fundamental assumptions: that market and technological conditions (expressed in a neoclassical production function) are the same for both enterprises; and that the capitalist firm has the objective of maximizing total profit while the cooperative has that of maximizing net income per unit of labour (or per member, if all workers are members).

The results, using this model, are the notorious 'perversities' about which so much has been written. First, the cooperative's short-term supply curve is negatively sloped, which is to say that when the price of the product rises, output decreases, and with it employment. Second, the cooperative's response to changing market conditions – input prices and the shape of the production function – contradicts the well-known laws of macroeconomic theory, all of which derive from the hypothesis that the objective of the firm is profit maximization.

A third perverse result was noted by Furubotn and Pejovich (1970), namely underinvestment by cooperatives, and hence their undercapitalization. The thesis is that whenever the time horizon of the median co-op member (the times they belong to the co-op) is shorter than the economic horizon of the investment (the time during which the investment generates positive returns), democratic governance on the one person, one vote principle will generate sub-optimal investment strategy and doom the cooperative to small size and progressive exclusion from the market. The explanation is simple. If the majority at the membership meeting are 'senior' members nearing the time when they will leave the co-op, they will presumably not vote in favour of long-term investment plans, to whose funding they must contribute but in whose benefits they will not share. This does not apply to the capitalist corporation's shareholder, who on deciding to leave the firm counts on selling their stake at a price that takes proportional account of the current value of the net future gains from the investment.

It is impossible to overestimate the damage that these findings have done to the image of the cooperative movement, which failed to respond promptly to the charge of lacking any theoretical argument to rebut these conclusions. The fact is that scientific work is only apparently innocuous because, as J.M. Keynes recalled, it tends to mould public opinion and ultimately to shape legislation. What actually underlies these 'perverse' results? Essentially, a simple methodological error: the operation of the capitalist firm is analysed in the framework of complete and perfect markets, while the cooperative is analysed on the assumption that there is no market for membership rights. Given such a market, the retiring co-op member could receive the present value of the future earnings of the enterprise's activity by selling their position to an incoming member or to the cooperative as such. Schlicht and Weizsacher (1977) were the first to show that there is perfect functional equivalence between the the stock exchange for capitalist firms and a market for memberhsip rights for cooperatives. Both underinvestment and Ward's perverse effects disappear if we posit such a market.

Here we must clear away two objections. The first question is whether a market in membership rights is compatible, in principle, with the nature of the cooperative enterprise. The answer is that it is. As long as control is solidly in the hands of the suppliers of labour, the cooperative identity is safe. As we know, the fundamental difference between the capitalist firm and the cooperative does not lie in the regime governing asset ownership – private in both cases – but in who ultimately controls the enterprise, the suppliers of capital or the suppliers of labour. It is important to observe that here we consider 'ultimate' control, because it is self-evident that in any but the smallest firm immediate control is in the hands of management; but in the capitalist firm, the managers are accountable to the holders of capital, whereas in the co-op they are accountable to the members.

We must simply acknowledge the existence of an asymmetry. Those who control the capitalist firm can 'adjust' to attain their profit-maximizing objective by operating in both capital and labour markets, while those who control the cooperative lack this possibility. This is why 'denying' the latter the possibility of using a market in membership rights inevitably produces the 'perverse' results described. Actually, in this sort of demonstration the conclusion is implicit in the model's initial hypotheses.

The second objection bears on the practical feasibility of such a market. We are fully aware of the obstacles to the creation of a market in cooperative membership positions, the most serious being cooperative workers' relative lack of financial resources. Dreze (1993) and Bowles and Gintis (1993) have pinpointed the capital constraint on worker members as the main cause of the practical difficulty of creating a market for membership rights. But this – important though it is – is a merely practical difficulty, while the results in question here derive from a theoretical argument; and at the level of theory, there is no impediment to the hypothesis that the cooperative enterprise can count on such a market.

The fact is that in the economic literature – even its best examples – the comparison between the two forms of enterprise is not conducted on an equal footing, that is, positing equal conditions. As Paul Samuelson made clear as far back as the 1950s, in a perfectly competitive environment and in equal conditions, it makes no difference 'who hires whom' (Samuelson, 1957), since an economy in which workers lease machinery and one in which capitalists rent workers will produce identical outcomes in terms of efficiency. Three decades later this conclusion was demonstrated in formal terms by Dreze (1989), but it has almost never been mentioned in the discussion over relative performance of the two types of enterprise.

6.2   THE NEO-INSTITUTIONAL APPROACH

Another intellectual approach – a sounder and more interesting one, in our view – cites the heterogeneity of members' preferences as the prime cause of cooperatives' greater fragility. Hart and Moore (1996) argue that because the democratic one person, one vote process will result in the victory of the option (an investment plan, say) that is favoured by the median member while the cost is sustained by all members equally, then the more the mean distribution of preferences diverges from the median, the greater the risk of relative inefficiency by comparison with the capitalist firm. In other words, whenever the membership meeting is divided into groups with sharply divergent viewpoints or interests, it is evident that unlike the capitalist corporation (with its one share, one vote principle), the cooperative inevitably risks paralysis or the de facto transfer of control to managers. The risk of a 'tyranny of the majority' is a real one in those co-ops where lack of strong identification with the organization's mission facilitates the creation of conflicting interest groups (whereas in the capitalist corporation the minority shareholder who is 'tyrannized' over can, at least in theory, leave the company without regrets).

Let us consider an example that illustrates the problems faced by a cooperative when members' preferences are not stable – the case in which a certain number of persons pay a certain amount to constitute the co-op's capital. The membership meeting then sets a compensation policy that depends on output level. Here, if the ability (or effort) of the median member is lower than that of the average member, this compensation policy will redistribute income from the more to the less productive members. But the more productive cannot leave the co-op, in practice, because this would entail forfeiting their initial investment. This is said to explain the relatively low earnings of cooperatives compared with capitalist firms and at the same time to highlight an obstacle to their growth, namely inefficient wage policy.

What does this example teach? Basically, that if we are to make conjectures on the performance of a cooperative, we must know the motivational structure of the people who decide to join it. Amartya Sen (1966) was the first to show how much what he called 'sympathy' – the weight that one member assigns, within his utility function, to the utility of the other members – affects the enterprise's performance. As we saw in Chapter 3, the decision to join a co-op is based not only on strict economic interest but also on a desire for positive freedom and a marked preference for fairness. It follows that if a person with these preferences elects to work in a cooperative, their behaviour cannot be the same as it would be in a capitalist firm.

An essay by Bacchiega and De Fraja (1999) helps clarify this point. They focus on the constitutional design, that is, the rules for producing a decision, in the two types of enterprise, assuming that technology, prices and personal utility functions are the same. The utility function comprises an individual consumption good, a local public good and a random variable. In a world of complete contracts, the choice of the firm's institutional arrangement would be perfectly irrelevant – there would always be a first-best solution, the one that maximizes the sum of individual utility functions. But if we have incomplete contracts, Bacchiega and De Fraja demonstrate that the cooperative produces underinvestment and poorer performance. Fundamentally, the reason is that the worker member is tempted to provide a smaller financial contribution than the capitalist shareholder to the enterprise's common action.

Intuitively, this result is explained by the fact – as we noted in Chapter 3 – that any common action always implies the production of some local public good, which inevitably raises the problem of free-riding. Cooperative members, even though they know that in the end free-riding (opportunistic behaviour) will give them a smaller benefit, owing to the insufficient output of the public good, have no incentive to increase their contribution and hence the volume of output. This is not the case in the capitalist firm, where a minority of shareholders – who, however, hold a majority of shares – can make decisions against the numerical majority. This means that shareholders have an incentive to contribute resources to the enterprise so as to 'buy the power to make decisions'. This incentive is what overcomes the problem of free-riding, which as such exists in capitalist enterprises as well. This means that what makes the difference between the capitalist firm and the cooperative enterprise is the asymmetrical holding of capital among the shareholders of the capitalist firm. In fact, if corporate shareholders all had the same stake, the same number of shares, they would behave like the members of a cooperative.

What can we conclude from these findings? First of all, that the specification of agents' utility function is crucial to the results one will get. Why in the world should the co-op member's be the same as the capitalist shareholder's? Certainly it is one thing to work for a firm in which you are controlled, quite another to do the same job where you yourself are in control. So while it is perfectly legitimate for the capitalist investor's utility function to be as outlined above, that of the cooperative worker-member cannot fail to include, as an additional argument, a parameter representing the weight attached to personal independence. Factoring this in, we would find that much more than the aim of 'buying the power to make decisions', the possibility of working in a gratifying environment can offset the danger of free-riding. For we know that the relationship between the individual worker and the firm goes beyond strictly economic exchange. It includes, for instance, a sense of belonging, which expresses people's fundamental need for identity, and this gives rise to a psychological interchange involving intangible but real elements such as loyalty, mutual trust and respect. No one can fail to see that, in considering the decision to join a cooperative, one simply cannot ignore these relational incentives. If material incentives alone are considered in comparing the two types of enterprise, then it goes without saying that the cooperative stands convicted – on the charge of inefficiency – before the hearing even begins.

The recent work of Henry Hansmann (1996) reinforces this conclusion. Asking why different types of enterprise should exist, he answers that this depends on the differring ability of the different stakeholders to minimize both the total costs for arriving at the contract (the costs of information, of contract drafting, of renegotiation and so on) and the costs of exercising ownership rights (the costs of controlling managers, of collective decision making, of risk taking). What determines whether the enterprise 'should' be structured as a capitalist firm or as a cooperative is therefore the differential ability of the various stakeholders to be efficient. By this logic, Hansmann conjectures that the cooperative is inherently transitory, bound in the long run to disappear or to converge on the capitalist form.

The argument runs as follows. As long as the quotas paid in by members or the reserves built up out of undistributed earnings are enough to finance expansion, the cooperative form poses no problem. But when the time comes to mobilize venture capital, potential outside investors, fearing abuses of power by the worker-members (who exercise ultimate control), will not put up the required amount of capital. This, it is argued, explains why cooperatives are so rare in the capital-intensive industries (steel, petrochemicals), where workers are 'too poor' to provide the necessary capital, or where leasing the needed capital equipment is too costly.

The capitalist firm also has serious, mirror-image problems: motivating those who work for it to make available the information they have, in particular their tacit knowledge, to optimize performance. Since people cannot be obliged to put their knowledge at the service of the firm, a climate of mutual trust is essential for good performance. Isn't this the key to the success of the Toyota method? What is the golden rule here? First of all is job security: the worker is unlikely indeed to invest in their own human capital and raise their skill level if the company offers no assurance that the work relationship will be lasting; instead, they will fear the lock-in effect. Second comes fairness in pay schemes within the firm. A vast body of empirical evidence tells us that people compare their own effort/compensation ratio with those of others in their reference group. Workers who perceive unfair treatment are unlikely to divulge tacit knowledge. Third is the social responsibility of the firm. The organization that acts for purposes that its workers consider socially significant will benefit from an appreciable increase in productivity and effort. Aren't these three components of the 'golden rule' precisely the features that mark the cooperative modus operandi?

It is easy to foresee the objection – why all this stress on tacit knowledge? Why should this be more important than factors like marketing, R&D or technology? Our answer is twofold. First, tacit knowledge, today, is more important strategically than codified knowledge (knowledge that can be verified by a third party and that can be transmitted in codes or protocols), which was crucial during the protracted period of domination by Fordist mass production methods. And second, a durable, sustainable competitive advantage can never stem from factors that can be replicated. Technology can be copied, just as marketing and advertising can be imitated. But the social relations and the relational goods generally engendered within a work environment cannot be replicated. Here lies the great comparative advantage of cooperative work organization. Admittedly, if co-op managers naively attempt to imitate the organization of the capitalist corporation and fail to capitalize on the particular strengths of the cooperative form, those strengths will remain sterile, and managers will resort to improbable financial operations simply to conceal their incapacity and even, at times, their outright irresponsibility.

The striking asymmetry between the inputs of capital and of labour must always be borne in mind. Where the ownership of capital assets can be readily transferred from one person to another, labour power – the ability to furnish work – is inalienable (Dow, 2003). It follows that an enterprise can get the capital it needs either from a stock of goods that it owns or from a flow of services via leasing. But labour services are available only in the form of a flow, as there is no 'stock' of workers (slavery being outlawed). And a person's work time cannot go beyond some natural limit, while there is no upper bound to the investor's wealth. Again, the person who supplies labour necessarily installs neighbourly relations with the other people who do so, and no one can be in two different work places at once, but the supplier of capital can be totally removed from the production process to which they gives their 'machinery' and can place machines in any number of different places at the same time. And above all, as Dow (2003) clearly argues, labour services are inherently heterogeneous, bound up as they are with the characteristics of the person providing them, while financial capital is homogeneous. In short, when the power of control is given to those who supply their labour, it is impossible to transfer control from A to B without replacing A's labour with B's. But in the capitalist corporation the voting rights embodied in shares can be switched from A to B with no change whatever in the firm's capital goods. To sum up, what makes the profound difference between capital and cooperative enterprises, and hence what causes the difference in relative efficiency, is the inalienability of the labour factor and the alienability of capital.

6.3   WHY STATIC EFFICIENCY IS AN UNSATISFACTORY YARDSTICK

Why is it unwise to take static efficiency as the sole yardstick for gauging the relative performance of capitalist and cooperative enterprises? There are three reasons. First, the contrary opinion of many observers notwithstanding, the notion of 'efficiency' is not value-neutral; as a term of discourse, it is not descriptive but prescriptive, not positive but normative. For it derives from the principle of utilitarianism, which is certainly not an economic but an ethical principle. Whether you take the Paretian or ordinal version or the cardinal version of efficiency defined as deviations from the first-best solution, it is still the assumption of utilitarian philosophy that must be adopted. How, then, can it be maintained that comparing the two types of enterprise in terms of efficiency is objective, value-neutral? The market economy, it is worth recalling, came into being long before utilitarianism, a point that it would be well to bear in mind today, now that utilitarianism itself is subject to philosophical criticism.

The second reason is that relying on strong idealistic motivations gives cooperatives a whole series of advantages. Yet in standard comparative analysis of the two forms of enterprise these advantages are never brought out, for the simple reason that the rational choice paradigm adopted cannot take agents' intrinsic motivations properly into account. In other words, instrumental rationality does not give adequate space to considerations of motivation and attitudes of mind or spirit. In fact, in this economic approach, the latter are reduced to specific arguments of the agent's utility function – exactly what motivations cannot stand. John Dewey, the founder of philosophical pragmatism, himself warned that human action cannot be explained strictly in terms of ends and beliefs – as if intrinsic motivations and the surrounding environment counted for nothing – but neither can it be explained as if ends and beliefs had no influence. Accordingly, when the famous article by Stigler and Becker (1977) maintains that changes in observed behaviour should be explained as a rational subject's response to changes in incentives alone, this demonstrates a kind of naive realism; in reality, incentives can never be defined independently of the motivations of the person to whom the incentives are directed. Consequently, if in calculating efficiency one excludes all the factors that motivate a person to become a member of a cooperative – capitalizing on personal initiative, the psychological advantage of reducing alienation, shared goals and common action, the preference for fairness – then clearly the comparison is biased in favour of the capitalist firm. That is, the disadvantages of co-ops are emphasized – above all those connected with raising capital – but the potential benefits are ignored.

The third reason, finally, is the failure to consider the positive social externalities produced by cooperative enterprise. The greatest of these is the democratization of society. If, as we think, democracy at the workplace strengthens and supports the democratization of political institutions – as Robert Dahl wrote in 1985 (p. 57), 'If democracy is justified in the government of the polity, then it is equally justified in the government of an enterprise' – and if we agree that democracy in society serves the purposes of economic growth, then a comparative analysis of the two forms of enterprise that fails to consider this is unacceptably partial and biased.

This is why the notion of dynamic efficiency must be the gauge if the comparison is to be meaningful or useful. To take the institutional set-up for the economic game as an unchangeable given that affects the outcome but is not affected by it is to suffer from severe 'short-termism'. We have long known that economic development depends on factors that are not strictly belonging to the economic sphere. Durkheim insisted that social values are not mere means at the disposal of economic agents, because society is always capable of obliging its members to conduct themselves in such a way as to neutralize the suggestions and recommendations that spring from a purely economic calculus.

This point implies a broader question. Underneath the capitalistic economy there lies a serious pragmatic – not, to be sure, logical – contradiction, one that the most discerning social scientists on both sides of the Atlantic have noted. The capitalist economy is certainly a market economy – as we have said, a set of institutional arrangements entailing two operative principles that are the keystone of modern society: freedom of action and enterprise and equality before the law. At the same time, however, capitalism's central institution, the capitalistic enterprise, has been constructed over the centuries on strictly hierarchical principles.

A system of production thus arose based on a central structure to which a certain number of persons voluntarily, in exchange for a monetary compensation, cede goods and services of their own, which once having entered the firm escape the control of those who supplied them. Economic history teaches how this came about, and also instructs us as to the enormous economic progress that this institutional arrangement produced. But the fact is that the contemporary transition – from the modern to a post-modern age – is marked by an increasingly widespread critique of the difficulty of making the democratic principle and the capitalistic principle co-exist. The main problem is the 'privatization of the public'. That is, capitalistic enterprises increasingly control the behaviour of individuals (who, be it noted, spend well over half their waking lives at work), removing them from self-government and the influence of other social institutions, notably the family. Such antidotes to the near-absolute power of the sovereign as the concepts of freedom of choice, tolerance, equality before the law, participation and others, coined and diffused in the era of civil humanism and reinforced during the Enlightenment, are taken over (in a revised form) by the capitalistic enterprise to transform persons from citizens – no longer subjects – into consumers of the goods and services the enterprise produces.

The contradiction is inherent in the fact that if there are sound reasons for wanting the greatest possible extension of the democratic principle, then there is a need to examine what happens within firms, not just between firms in the marketplace. This is the importance of the positive social externalities engendered by cooperatives. No society can ever be fully democratic as long as the democratic principle is applied only in the polity. A good society in which to live will not constrain its members to embarassing disassociation: democratic as citizen and voter, non-democratic as worker and consumer (Zamagni, 2006).

One wonders: how can we explain the fact that this point has virtually never been considered in economics? The answer is an unhappy confusion between a partnership or professional contract, on the one hand, and a labour contract on the other. In law, in a partnership contract two or more parties join in common action with the aim of sharing the surplus (net product); in a professional contract one person undertakes to provide a piece of work for another with no hierarchical subordination; but in the labour contract, one party (the employee) renounces their own decision-making autonomy for a specified period of time in favour of the other party (the employer), in exchange for a compensation determined in advance, independent of the firm's results. What is more, whereas in the company contract decision-making power is shared among the partners, who exercise it as they themselves determine, and in the project contract, although the nature of the services and the remuneration are indeed set in advance, the way in which services are supplied is decided independently by the worker, the employment contract does not involve the exchange of defined goods or services but the pledge of obedience; wages, that is, constitute the price of waiving the intangible good known as personal liberty.

In this light, it is easy to see the *raison d'être* of the cooperative enterprise. By putting workers in a position to control their productive activity, the co-op applies the principles of equality and liberty that animate the market economy with the enterprise itself. In principle at least, the cooperative thus resolves our pragmatic contradiction. If autonomy, liberty, is taken as a value in itself, regardless of whether it leads to greater or lesser economic results, then it is clear why the cooperative is the form of choice of people who put personal freedom and independence at the top of their scale of values.

This suggests what we consider as perhaps the most plausible of the many explanations for the limits in the diffusion of cooperatives around the world. That is, the passion for positive liberty is not yet most people's most prized value. This is no grounds for surprise or scandal, because liberty belongs to the category of superior goods. In economics a superior good is one whose income elasticity is greater than one. This is tantamount to saying that it is only above a certain income threshold, only when essential needs are satisfied, that a person can be in a position to assign increasing importance to the good of liberty. So we can conclude that the more broadly our society extends conditions in which liberty can become a superior good, the more the cooperative form of enterprise will discover new reasons for being (Mazzoli and Zamagni, 2005).

7. Cooperative governance

7.1 COOPERATIVES IN THE AGE OF FINANCIALIZATION

That the cooperative movement today is at a crossroads is common knowledge. The observation is heavily laden with significance, indicating the great vitality that this form of enterprise has won in the economic battlefield. At the same time, however, its very successes raise new, worrying questions. Is it still possible that in today's new conditions the cooperative enterprise can continue to do well – as well as its capitalist counterpart – and also to serve its other purposes? Or, to state the issue from a different angle, is there something to the argument that in the age of the financialization of the economy there is just no room for enterprises for which the social dimension is central? On proper consideration, questions like this all point, directly or indirectly, to two main themes: how to administer cooperatives and how to finance their growth without endangering their special identity.

To administer a cooperative in a correct way requires two conditions: on the one hand, the line of communication among worker-members must be rendered accessible; on the other hand, there must be a commitment to the practice of equity, avoiding subjection and exploitation. Let's try to clarify. Communication is different than information. While complete information is all that is needed to solve the problem of coordination of decisions, cooperation presupposes that a particular form of participatory democracy is put into place: the exercise among the members of the firm of the option of voice. It is to Albert Hirschman that we owe the important distinction between exit and voice, and the affirmation that, while the former would find its ideal-type place of application in the economic sphere, the latter would find space, instead, in the political sphere. The unique significance of the cooperative way of doing business is that it extends the exercise of voice to the sphere of economic relations. As is known, the deliberative process postulates the possibility of self-correction, that each subject allows for, *ab imis,* the possibility of changing their preferences in light of the reasons adopted by the others. The deliberative method, it is implied, is not compatible with those who, in the name of power hierarchy, declare themselves impermeable to the arguments of others.

It is for this reason that deliberation presupposes, necessarily, communication. According to Cohen (1989), cooperation is based on 'deliberation focused on the common good' in which the participants declare themselves disposed to putting into play their own initial preferences, because 'the relevant preferences and convictions are those that emerge from, or are confirmed by, means of deliberation' (p. 69). A cooperative that does not comprehend this unique aspect and that, in the name of efficiency, apes the modus operandi of the capitalist firm – in which by definition no deliberative process can find its place – is condemned to euthanasia. Also the cooperative firm is much better equipped than its twin capitalist firm to take advantage of the potential of the network as an endogenous form of organization which allows users to benefit from dynamic externalities, strategic complementarities and cumulative phenomena. It is true that to build a network structure coordination is all that is required. But it is equally true that the network structures provide the maximum advantage when the three conditions of which Bratman (1999) speaks are satisfied.

The other condition for a correct administration of a cooperative is the commitment to internal equity. The freedom of members to join a cooperative is justified first by the goal of barring any subjugation or exploitation. The idea of cooperation distinguishes itself from that of coordination because, while the latter postulates hierarchy, the former presupposes equal dignity among the subjects and the environments in which they operate. Cooperation – observes John Rawls – demands much more than coordination, in as much as it is based on rules and procedures that are accepted and made by all of the participants. It is of course true that in every common action, and therefore in each firm, someone who exercises the function of command so that individual wishes might converge is required. But while in the capitalistic firm command comes down through the power hierarchy, and can be applied in a more or less authoritarian way depending on personal characteristics, in the cooperative firm command is associated with authority in such a way that no one can impose on others their own way of interpreting the common action. It follows that the cooperative that founded its governance structure on the hierarchical model, instead of on that of authority, would miss the most precious occasion for valorizing its identity specificity.

As Besley and Ghatak (2004) suggest, a 'mission' consists of a unity of attributes of a project in which those who take part evaluate its success beyond the monetary income that they receive. In this sense, the cooperative can be seen as a mission-oriented organization that draws power from the motivations of its agents. Motivated is the agent that pursues a particular end because they know that there is an intrinsic benefit in doing a certain thing or in behaving in a certain way. Clearly, the existence of a mission, while reducing the need to negotiate pecuniary incentive schemes, also increases the importance – for the goal of optimizing the effort of the agents – of the non-pecuniary aspects of the firm's organizational structure.

In symbolic terms, this means assuming, for the generic subject i, a utility function of the type: $U_i = a\ w_i + (1 - a)\ m_i$, where w_i denotes pecuniary remuneration, m_i intrinsic motivation and $a\ (0 < a < 1)$ the weight given to the first component and $(1 - a)$ the weight attributed to the second. Now, because intrinsic motivations differ, in general, from person to person, one of the two scenarios will result: either the mission-oriented firm, as is the cooperative, is able to organize this diversity and therefore will be able to make consistent productivity improvements, or is not able to do this and will fall victim to paralyzing conflicts. This is why the manager of the cooperative must know how 'to do well' as much as his capitalist counterpart and, in addition, do more; that is, they must know how to find the optimal mix of w and m, material incentives and relational incentives. If the cooperative manager, overcome by a craving for imitation due to a sort of inferiority complex, insists only on the variable w, they will end up provoking the crowding out effect of which Frey (1997) speaks: the intrinsic motivations are anaesthetized by the extrinsic motivations.

Gibbons (1998), in a different context, does not exclude this eventuality at all when he writes: 'A troubling possibility is that management practices based on [traditional] economic models can reduce or even destroy non-economic realities like intrinsic motivation and social relations' (p. 130). It would be truly paradoxical if, in an historical period like the current one in which the most celebrated studies of the capitalistic mode of organization are discovering that economic sustainability cannot be assured through controls and material incentives alone, the leaders of the cooperative movement were to miss the occasion to utilize the specificities of the cooperative form of enterprise to reach objectives that, through coordination only, are not possible. As Falk and Kosfeld (2004) have recently demonstrated experimentally, the use of material incentives, insofar as this is a sign of distrust of the agent on the part of the principal, significantly reduces the willingness of the former to act in the interests of the latter. The use of incentives backfires, so to speak, against the principal, and the agent's performance is inferior with respect to that which would have otherwise been obtained.

This is because giving trust increases the self-esteem (the self-esteem of which Adam Smith spoke) of those who receive it. This, while improving productivity, reduces the risk that is always associated with the attribution of trust (Pelligra, 2007). As is well known, the labour relationship between firm and worker can assume the form of the so-called 'social exchange' or 'market exchange'. In the first case immaterial elements like fairness, honesty and reciprocity enter into play which are not negotiable because they are not verifiable. In the second case, instead, the exchange is based on those elements that fall under incentive systems of one type or another. We well know that different types of work relationships lead to great differences in firm performance. But it is evident that the worker will accept entering into a 'social exchange' instead of a 'market exchange' only if the firm will appear to them as a moral subject that declares to accept putting into practice the cooperative principle which allows workers to choose freely those projects that maximize their benefits (Aghion and Tirole, 1997).

The second challenge that cooperatives have to face today is how to finance their growth. First we can observe that the issue mainly involves worker co-ops, farmer cooperatives less so and consumer co-ops only marginally. This is not hard to explain. Where for the latter and for small co-ops self-financing through indivisible, undistributed earnings with their favourable tax regime, together with membership loans and careful cash management, is sufficient, in practice, to meet funding needs, this is not the case with the larger worker cooperatives, which ordinarily have capital-intensive production processes. These cooperatives' members are economically weak, which simply precludes their providing sufficient capital. This is true of the other types of cooperative as well, but in consumer co-ops the large number of members at least partly compensates for their limited ability (or desire) to subscribe equity capital. Nor is it thinkable that the common practice of earmarking rebates for capital increases, increasing each member's quota instead of distributing them in cash, is the solution. Not only because of the modest size of these amounts in absolute terms but also because rebates are not in fact the member's right, but a decision that must be taken by the membership meeting.

Let us consider the problem of co-ops' finance in the Italian case.

7.2   LEGISLATIVE EFFORTS IN ITALY TO INCREASE CO-OPS' FUNDING BEFORE THE 2003 LAW

The first, classic, instrument to fund a cooperative is the issue of cooperative shares subscribed by the members. In Italy this is subject to a twofold constraint: no member could hold shares worth more than 100 000 euros (to ensure that no member could, in spite of the formal maintenance of the one person, one vote principle, acquire de facto power at the membership meeting); and, as laid down by Article 2530 of the Civil Code, 'The quotas or shares of members cannot be sold with effect on the society if the sale is not authorized by the directors.' This second constraint is more stringent still, because it simply precludes the institution of a true market in co-op shares. Taken together, the two constraints guarantee that the issue of shares for members – the main way in which capitalistic firms fund themselves – will never satisfy the cooperative's need for funds.

Legislation subsequent to the Basevi Law – in particular, the Visentini law of 1983 – did, however, allow cooperatives to constitute (or purchase) joint stock companies (or limited partnerships), including listed ones, under their control. The co-op, if it holds a 51 per cent stake, can raise funds by placing the remaining 49 per cent with other investors. This is the idea behind the creation of the cooperative groups. It enables the parent co-op to raise more investment capital through the subsidiaries. Law 59/1992 introduced new financial instruments: cooperative preferential shares and investor member shares. Preferential shares, intended to finance corporate restructuring, do not carry voting rights but are privileged in terms of profit distribution and equity reimbursement in the case of liquidation of the co-op. The holders of these shares do not take part in the appointment of directors, and they have the advantage of remaining anonymous. Given these features and the impossibility of creating a true market in these instruments, it is easy to see why they had no success.

The investor member shares did slightly better. Unlike the preferential shares, they circulate freely and the return on them is not subject to the limits that apply to cooperative members. Investor members can designate some directors (a minority) and have voting rights, but no more than a third of the total. However investor member shares cannot be listed – co-op shares are subject to constraints on transferability – so they too proved a substantial failure. In formal terms, their failure was softened only by the fact that most of them were taken up by the promotion funds of the umbrella cooperative organizations, also instituted by Law 59/1992. These funds are non-profit public limited companies whose corporate purpose is the promotion of cooperatives. The legitimacy of their actions is subject to the oversight of the Ministry of Labour together with the cooperative umbrella organizations.

No wonder then, given the essence of the cooperative movement, that the expectations for these cooperative capital instruments were disappointed. The cooperative member cannot be reduced to a mere financier, which means that the concept of the 'investor member' is basically an oxymoron. But if this is so, the question is how it was possible to raise such hopes in the first place. In our view, the source of the problem is the error induced by the thesis that the mutualistic benefit for the member derives from a separate exchange contract, distinct from the contract binding them with the cooperative. For if the exchange contract is in addition, then in principle it is separable from the original contract that gave rise to the cooperative; at this point, it becomes perfectly justified to create ad hoc members by issuing investment shares.

In other words, if it is admissible for the mutual purposes of the co-op to be separate, embodied in an exchange contract distinct from the articles of constitution, then it is recognized that one may become a member of a cooperative before practising mutualism; and hence, that that aim itself is secondary. The indefensibility of any such thesis is self-evident, however, because mutual aid is an integral part of the identity of the cooperative member: I am member of a cooperative only insofar as I practise and benefit from mutualistic exchange. While the legal fiction of the additional contract may serve to resolve certain specific problems – such as the application of labour legislation to worker-members – where it is intended as a fund-raising mechanism for cooperatives it results in failure and frustration.

The situation is no better when we examine cooperatives' instruments for raising debt capital. First of all, bonds. Before the 1998 law the prevalent opinion was that co-ops could not issue bonds, because they had variable capital and consequently could not guarantee repayment. This belief has now been definitively disproved: cooperatives may issue bonds for an amount up to their equity capital and own funds. Credit Unions can exceed that ceiling, thanks to the intelligent creation of a consortium guaranteeing the repayment of all bondholders. This is a sort of collective guarantee, which other types of cooperative could also exploit, in principle; in practice, however, it is hindered by the diversity of the co-ops in size and sector.

A second instrument for debt-based fund raising, of course, is membership or cooperative group loans (the latter being considerably less common). For cooperatives with more than 50 members this debt is limited to three times the co-op's equity capital plus legal reserves and the reserves available as recorded in the latest financial statement; the ceiling is raised to five times that amount when the loan is backed by special guarantees. The individual member, whose loan cannot exceed a set ceiling, enjoys tax allowance on their interest income, making the proposition more attractive to members. For the co-op itself, however, things stand differently. The consumer co-ops, with their 6.5 million members, can raise substantial funds in this manner, but for the rest the costs of loan management often exceed the benefits. Another difficulty is that ordinary commercial banks are obviously not happy to see membership loans becoming widespread, as this takes liquidity away from their own sphere of business. True, the 1993 Consolidated Law on Banking exempts loans from cooperative members from the rule prohibiting all organizations except banks from raising repayable funds from the public. At the same time, however, some observers wonder – in the light of recent position statements by the European Commission, above all – how long this exemption can be maintained.

Finally, there is bank lending. Today the verdict on the effectiveness of this means of raising debt capital is mixed. On the one hand, the existence of indivisible reserves makes the co-op more creditworthy, with the consequent benefit in terms of lower debt service costs. But, on the other hand, the recent Basel II capital accords cast a deep shadow over the practical possibility of cooperatives to get much assistance from commercial banks. This is because the risk evaluation models adopted under Basel II refer to the probability of default of a profit-maximizing enterprise – that is, a capitalistic firm. It follows that the economic parameters of these credit models are those typical of capitalistic corporations. And if such indicators as net operating profit, dividends, return on equity (ROE) and so on are relevant to the default risk of a capitalist corporation, they are certainly not useful for evaluating cooperatives. No one, therefore, can fail to see that a distorted application of risk manage-

ment systems may severely damage cooperatives, possibly even result-
ing in credit rationing. Let us note, in passing, that this is one further
instance in which the purported neutrality of certain analytical tools –
here, estimated probability of default – actually conceals definite value
choices.

7.3 ITALIAN COOPERATIVES UNDER THE REFORMED COMPANY LAW

What are the implications of the foregoing? Taken as a group, the instruments we have discussed for raising funds, whether equity or debt capital, are insufficient to furnish cooperatives with the resources needed for
growth. And in a market economy this outright discrimination is simply
unacceptable. But – some will object – aren't the co-ops' tax benefits an
offsetting discrimination in their favour? The answer is no, and for the
simplest possible reason: cooperatives have their own statutes and by-
laws under civil law, setting them apart from for-profit companies, so
that the special tax measures are not selective – as defined, say, by
Article 87 of the European Union Treaty – and thus cannot be termed
state aid.

Recognizing this helps us to see why the company law reform of
2003 introduced new financial instruments, which are not yet actually in
being or even imminent. These are subordinated bonds, that is, bonds
having the lowest priority, redeemed only once all other creditors have
been paid; convertible bonds and quasi-shares. With these new instruments, a limited company can issue securities carrying capital and
administrative but not voting rights. The holders can, however, vote on
specific items and can also designate an independent director.

With specific reference to cooperatives, the 2003 reform of the Civil
Code paradoxically relaxes the requirements for authorization. Article
2526 reads: 'The statutes may provide for the issue of financial instruments under the rules that apply to joint stock companies.' But actually
the holders of the co-ops' financial instruments already have broader
powers than the bondholders of limited companies. The latter neither
vote nor designate a director; the former can have as much as a third of
the voting rights and designate up to a third of the board of directors.

To grasp the why and wherefore of this measure, let us look at the
truly major novelty of the reform: the distinction between cooperatives
with predominantly mutual purposes and others. Under Article 2512:

'Cooperatives with predominantly mutual purposes, in accordance with the type of mutual exchange, are those that exercise their activity primarily on behalf of their members, consumers, or users of goods and services.' This means that for consumer co-ops, the users must mostly be members; most of mutual banks' fund raising and lending must be with members; worker co-ops must rely mainly on member workers and so on. The next two Articles specify the criteria for determining whether a co-op has or lacks predominantly mutual purposes. For instance, for consumer co-ops revenue from the sale of goods to members must account for more than 50 per cent of total revenue. And Article 2514 lays down that primarily mutual co-ops must include in their by-laws the well-known requirements of the Basevi Law: ban on dividends larger than the top rate on postal savings bonds plus 2.5 percentage points; ban on remuneration of financial instruments subscribed by members exceeding the ceiling on dividends by more than two points; ban on distributing indivisible reserves to members; and in the event of liquidation (or conversion into a limited company), obligation to devolve assets to mutual promotion funds.

In exchange for these obligations and limits, these primarily mutual purpose cooperatives enjoy certain tax benefits. They still make up 90 per cent of all Italian co-ops. The others are cooperatives that can distribute their reserves to their members, distribute unlimited dividends and assign their residual assets to the individual members in case of liquidation. That is, while these enterprises still have democratic governance and so continue to be considered cooperatives, their purpose is to make profits; this, for instance, is the case of the popular banks.

The spontaneous question is how a cooperative whose purposes are not prevalently mutual can still be called a cooperative. The question is prompted by the fact that the 2003 reform recognizes that such cooperatives too perform the social function referred to in Article 45 of the Constitution. Yet one of the requirements specified in that Article is the absence of the profit motive ('without private speculative ends'). The question is at the centre of a lively debate, and still far from being settled.

It may be helpful, in this context, to compare the Italian cooperative lacking primarily mutual purposes with the American 'new generation cooperative' (NGC), a model that arose in the early 1990s and is especially common in farming and food processing (Schaffner, 2004). There are three main points that distance the new generation co-op from the principles espoused by the International Cooperative Alliance in 1995.

First, entry into the NGC is closed, so the open door principle is violated. Entry barriers prevent the risk of an excessively diversified membership base, which as Chapter 6 showed has been the cause of considerable inefficiency. Second, there is no ceiling on members' contributions of capital, which means that a large proportion of earnings is distributed. Third, members' quotas (or shares) can be freely traded at a price reflecting the market value of the enterprise.

The reason for the creation of the new generation cooperative is twofold. On the one hand it minimizes the costs of collective decision making and, even more importantly, makes it easier for members to control management. And, on the other hand, it combats membership free-riding. In the traditional farmer cooperatives – where, be it noted, farmers are not obligated to deal with the co-op – the members will be sorely tempted to sell their crops to another enterprise while still bene-fiting from the positive externality of the cooperative's presence, which keeps private monopolists from driving prices too low. In the NGC the member is bound to the co-op both by a long-term marketing contract and by a substantial equity stake.

7.4   COOPERATIVES AND DEMOCRATIC STAKEHOLDING

We are now in a position to draw some relevant conclusions. In leaving the use of the new financial instruments made available to the discretion of the cooperative's own by-laws, the law raises an extremely delicate problem. How can a co-op – one with primarily mutual purposes – have as subsidiary a joint stock company (staffed by non-members), or use the new instruments (even entering them as 'equity') without eroding its own cooperative identity? True, limits are set on the powers of the subscribers of these instruments; but there is no limit on the size of their stake. True, the mutual purpose of the genuine cooperative members is not eliminated in order to allow profit making by the new investors; but isn't there nevertheless the risk that the profit motive will crowd out the mutual purpose? The questions, we can see, are fundamental; they point to an apparent dilemma: retaining the cooperative identity (and forgoing growth) or expanding (at the cost of losing that identity). On closer inspection, however, things are not so tragic as they might seem, or as they are often described by less than disinterested observers.

First of all, the very idea of this trade-off must be rejected as false and misleading. Let us employ a very well-known analogy. In 1975 the eminent economist Arthur Okun published the influential *The Big Trade-off*, whose thesis was that the modern economy poses an unavoidable alternative between efficiency and equity. Greater efficiency comes at the cost of less social equity, and vice versa. Okun was intrigued by such questions as: how much efficiency must a society forgo in order to improve equity? Is it better to expand the scope of the logic of exchange of equivalents – directed to efficiency – or to assign more power to government, which can act to impose greater equity? Today, although the demonstration has not gained the widespread notoriety it deserves, we know that this is simply not the way matters stand. Instead, a fairer distribution of income favours the dynamic efficiency of the economy as a whole, while greater dynamic efficiency itself presupposes greater distributive equity. And if we refer to the fundamental difference between the capitalistic and the cooperative enterprise (see Chapter 6), we can see why the trade-off between cooperative identity and growth is not inevitable. This does not mean, of course, that it is impossible, or that it has not had to be grappled with in practice.

A second observation further attenuates this dilemma. Admittedly, the subsidiary joint stock company (whether listed or not) cannot have the same objective function as the parent cooperative. But this certainly does not imply that the cooperative group must replicate the governance of the capitalistic corporate group, nor that its strategy must rest on the principle of maximizing 'shareholder value'. If, as Sacconi (2006) notes, the cooperative group attains excellence in corporate social responsibility – that is, management's discharging real responsibilities with respect to the entire, broad range of stakeholders – then the conflict of interest between shareholders and members vanishes. To prevent misunderstanding, we are not saying that this is easy; nor do we want to judge some embryonic experiences in this area. All we intend to do is indicate that there is no reason, in principle, why the cooperative group cannot avoid the trade-off trap.

To this end, however, two conditions must be fulfilled. First, there must be no succumbing to the temptation of dual morality, that is, the idea of running the cooperative group according to a different, indeed diametrically opposite, logic from the parent co-op. Sooner or later, such dual business logic will always produce perverse results, because the management of the group would be acting as a sort of double agent. It would have two agency relationships with two different principals: one with the shareholder investors and one with the cooperative members.

As the objective functions of the two principals are mutually incompatible, in the long run the management will inevitably give in to the requests of the shareholder investors, as they are the ones who can credibly threaten the very survival of the group. For their purposes are not mutual and they will never set any limits to profit maximization beyond those of the law – or at the very most, standard notions of corporate social responsibility.

The second necessary condition is that the top officers uphold the strategy of democratic stakeholding, to supersede managerial stakeholding, a governance model that leaves it to the CEO (at the most, the board of directors) to reconcile the various interests at stake in more or less paternalistic fashion (Zamagni, 2006). Democratic stakeholding seeks to offer everyone engaged in relations with the group the real (not virtual) ability to take part in the decision-making process, in forms that vary with the situation. It is worth stressing that in this regard transparency of communication – correct and truthful information – is not sufficient. Nor is consultation enough (notoriously, many meetings realize direct democratic participation in appearance only). What is required is management accountability to all stakeholders. Unquestionably, this is no easy assignment; but it is certainly possible, as long as we free ourselves from the crippling heritage of ideology. For instance, voting by mail has no contraindications; yet the new rules only enable but do not require cooperatives to institute the procedure.

The foregoing makes it clear why the proposal advanced by some – to solve the problem of cooperative governance by applying the model of the foundation – is unacceptable in Italy. Quite simply, the idea is to place the ownership of each co-op in the hands of a private-law foundation. The foundation would manage its shareholding under mutual principles, while the operation of the enterprise itself would be entrusted to an entity following the capitalist rule. In practical terms, this was the procedure instituted by law in 1992 to privatize Italy's savings banks and pawn banks while safeguarding the non-profit nature of the assets accumulated to that point. This operation, though open to criticism on a number of points, did at least produce a non-profit solution – the foundation – that was comparable in nature to its predecessor institution (also a non-profit institution) although different in operational terms. To clarify our thinking, let us consider the case of a successful worker cooperative that wants to expand and in order to raise the necessary funds decides to turn its assets over to a limited company that will hire the worker members. Meanwhile, the co-op becomes a foundation that holds a majority stake in the company and manages it in keeping with the criteria laid down in the act of transformation. As a non-profit institution, the foundation can allocate its dividend income to strengthen or promote the cooperative cause.

This superficially attractive hypothesis is open to a twofold critique. First, it would transform the original cooperative members into wage workers for the new company and simultaneously members of the new foundation. From the standpoint of our analysis here, this would represent serious regression: from co-owners to wage workers. What would become of these former co-op members, now wage earners, if corporate operations should deprive them of their jobs? What is the point of continued membership in the cooperative foundation if it no longer enables the workers to protect their jobs? That, after all, was the original motivation behind the entire cooperative movement. And second, the newly formed joint stock company would be given the assets of the disbanding cooperative. But the value of the enterprise being transferred is itself the product of a history, variable in length and amplitude to be sure, of funds being allocated to tax-favoured indivisible reserves. In a sense, in view of the fiscal advantages received, the value of these assets is at least partly ascribable to the entire national community. The citizenry as a whole would be perfectly justified in contesting the alteration of the original motivation for those benefits.

In reality, in our hypothetical case, the operation would produce a joint stock company and a non-profit institution, eliminating any form of cooperative enterprise. The dissimilarity between cooperative foundations and the foundations formed in Italy out of the privatization of savings banks is self-evident. The savings banks and pawn banks were themselves originally not-for-profit enterprises, hiving off a for-profit part; but with the creation of the cooperative foundation, what remains after such a hiving-off is an institution substantially different from the parent body. If carried out, the plan for the cooperative foundation would have only one, inevitable outcome: the end of the cooperative movement and of cooperative enterprise. Now one may perfectly well take that as one's aim. But those who do should at least have the intellectual honesty to acknowledge explicitly that that is indeed the ultimate consequence of their plan.

8. Conclusion

The meaning – the ultimate sense – of the road we have travelled lies in one key question. Namely, what can we do to enable the market to serve – as it did, at least in part, at its dawning in the fifteenth century – to strengthen social bonds by fostering an economic space where those who wish can practise, and thus regenerate, the very values without which the market could not offer its best side, or even truly exist – mutual trust, reciprocity, equity, democracy? Seeking the answer to this question, one unavoidably recognizes the importance, within our advanced economies, of the cooperative form of enterprise, not an antagonist but an alternative to the capitalist corporation. That is, one must acknowledge the need to maintain a living space within and not outside the market, occupied by people and institutions whose economic action is inspired by the mutual philosophy. Because participation in that space cannot be detached from the associative link that motivates it, mutual cooperation forms part of the behavioural principle of reciprocity. Reciprocity, however, must not be mistaken for the exchange of equivalents, which is actually the cornerstone of capitalistic conduct. The essential aspect of reciprocity in a relationship is that the transfer is not dissociable from the underlying human relations. That is, the object of the transaction cannot be separated from the personal identity of those who carry it out. So under reciprocity exchange ceases to be anonymous and impersonal. This is why we have stressed, repeatedly, that mutual exchange – that is, reciprocity – is the essential connotation of the cooperative form of enterprise.

What are the conditions in which a phenomenon like cooperative enterprise can attain a size such as to make it a permanent, equilibrating component of the market? Let us set out the three conditions that seem to us most urgently indispensable. The first is cultural. It is necessary that educational institutions acknowledge and teach that economic conduct founded upon principles other than self-interest and the exchange of equivalents may also be successful. We know that fulfilling this condition will not be easy. In fact, the economic science of the last couple of centuries – assisted by contractualist political philosophy – has taught us all to think that there is no escape from the choice between two radically different conceptions of the market. One sees the marketplace as the arena of exploitation, the domination of the strong over the weak, and accordingly judges the expansion of the market space as the prime cause, to use Karl Polanyi's powerful image, of the 'desertification' of society. The other conception sees the continuous spread of the capitalist market, thus the ever more pervasive logic of profit, as the solution to all social ills – to use another striking, frequently used image, a 'rising tide raises all the boats' (Sen, 1983).

Yet it is quite simply false – mistaken – to see such pairs as freedom and justice, efficiency and equity, self-interest and solidarity, and independence and belonging as dichotomies, irreconcilable antagonists. We know, from our own personal experience, that it is wrong to see the strengthening of a sense of belonging as a necessary diminution of the individual's independence; any advance in efficiency as a threat to equity; any bettering of private interests as undercutting the common good. The intellectual tradition of civic economy, rooted in civil humanism – a quintessentially Italian school of thought that takes a back seat neither to that of political economy nor to that of the social market economy – teaches that we can have human society and fraternity inside a normal market economy, if only we want to.

The second of our three conditions concerns the demand side of the economy. An intriguing new feature of the current period is the tendency towards an inversion of the historical dependency of consumption on production. Notwithstanding a series of contradictory elements, consumption now appears to be in a position to guide production, a situation that John Stuart Mill had intuited in the mid-nineteenth century with his celebrated reference to 'the sovereignty of the consumer.' Exercising the possibility of substituting one good or service on the market for another, the consumer undertakes a selection of firms, choosing to buy from one or from another, just as the businessman, as Marshall would later say, chooses among the factors of production. True enough, the consumer has never been sovereign, and is not today, at least not fully. But it is also true that in today's historical conditions consumers are increasingly keen to know and appreciate not only the technical characteristics of any good they intend to purchase but also how it was produced.

The fact is that before being a consumer, one is perforce a buyer, that is, a person who collects information on the story incorporated in a product. And a novel development of our time is the rise of the 'socially responsible consumer'. That is, social responsibility is incumbent not only on corporations; the citizen as consumer cannot feel exempt from the civic duty of using their purchasing power – the key word here is 'power' – for whatever purposes they themselves deem worthy and important. It is this consideration, not mere economic interest, that explains the extraordinary success of consumer cooperatives in Italy and in other places. So the more citizen-consumers become sovereign, and thus the more they become aware of their social responsibility, the greater will be the scope for the growth of cooperation.

Our third condition, finally, is political and institutional. Economic history teaches that moral and civic progress requires a society in which different types of enterprise can operate within the market on a substantially equal footing. The reason is clear enough. An avowedly liberal social order cannot require that all individuals adhere to the same motivational and value system, that is, that they have the same preferences. Thus an economic and institutional order that, de facto, favours the capitalist corporation is anti-liberal and hence self-contradictory; what is more, it deprives itself of the ability to use the variety of types of enterprise for its own, self-proclaimed objectives. Here we are referring to such ends as a more equitable distribution of income, greater dynamic efficiency, a higher rate of social capital accumulation and a more robust democracy. It has been demonstrated, as we have sought to show in this volume, that where the presence of the cooperative movement is strongest, other things being equal, the indicators of development and welfare are higher.

Consider the semantic slippage affecting the usage of terms like 'public' and 'social' in the current political debate. 'Public' denotes the whole, the general interest. But 'social' now refers to the marginal segments of the population, and in fact the term 'social policy' means measures in favour of the poor. It having been discovered that wealth is not self-propagating, that it does not spread sideways but only moves upwards, political programmes are now drafted in the name of the 'public', which is to say the entire community. In this way inequality is flanked by distinctions: the poor and the rich, those who receive public assistance and those who do not, are divided not only by economic inequality but by a difference in status. Yet no genuinely liberal social order, on pain of disintegration, can permit the inevitable inequality between individuals to degenerate into differences in status, into discrimination (Sen, 1999).

This is why any society interested in progress needs a market that has room for enterprises whose action has pro-social motivations – enterprises like cooperatives. Hence the urgent need to make it understood that the purpose of political action is not simply to enact measures in favour of certain economic agents such as to preserve the given economic and institutional order, but also to favour the flowering of agents embodying a different mode of economic action. If, as we believe, a democratic economy is one in which several principles of economic organization can thrive and in which legal and political institutions do not favour one over the others, then the cooperative movement can only welcome any and all initiatives to expand the space of liberty.

The study of the cooperative economy, after 160 years, is still practically embryonic, but we are convinced that it will grow to become an effective carrier of contagion. As T.S. Eliot observes, you can't build a tree, you can only plant one, tend it, and wait for it to sprout in due time. You can, however, speed up its growth. For unlike animals, who live in time but have no time, human beings have the ability to alter their times.

References

Aghion, P. and J. Tirole (1997), 'Formal and real authority in organizations', *Journal of Political Economy*, **105**, 1–29.

Bacchiega, A. and G. De Fraja (1999), 'Constitutional design and investment in cooperatives and investor-owned enterprises', Department of Economics, University of York, March.

Battilani, P. (1999), *La creazone di un moderno sistema di imprese*, Bologna: Il Mulino.

Battilani, P. and G. Bertagnoni (eds) (2007), *Competizione e valorizzazione del lavoro. La rete cooperativa del Consorzio Nazionale Servizi*, Bologna: Il Mulino.

Ben-Ner, A., W.A. Burns, G. Dow and L. Putterman (2000), 'Employee ownership: an empirical exploration', in M. Blair and T. Kochan (eds), *The New Relationship: Human Capital in the American Corporation*, Washington, DC: Brookings Institute Press, pp. 194–210.

Bertagnoni, G. (ed.) (2004), *Una storia di qualità. Il gruppo Granarolo fra valori etici e logiche di mercato*, Bologna: Il Mulino.

Besley, T. and M. Ghatak (2004), 'Competition and incentives with motivated agents', CEPR, 4641.

Birchell, J. (1994), *Coop: The People's Business,* Manchester: Manchester University Press.

Bonin, J.P. and L. Putterman (1987), *Economics of Cooperation and the Labour-managed Economy*, London: Harwood.

Bonin J., D. Jones and L. Putterman (1993), 'Theoretical and empirical studies of producer cooperatives', *Journal of Economic Literature*, **31**, 1290–320.

Borzaga, C. and A. Ianes (2006), *L'economia della solidarietà. Storia e prospettive della cooperazione sociale*, Rome: Donzelli.

Bowles S. and H. Gintis (1993), 'A political and economic case for the democratic enterprise', *Economics and Philosophy*, **9**, 75–100.

Bratman, M. (1999), 'Shared cooperative activity', in M. Bratman, *Faces of Intention*, Cambridge: Cambridge University Press, p. 94.

Bruni, L. (2006), *Reciprocità*, Milan: Bruno Mondadori.

Bruni, L. and S. Zamagni (2007), *Civil Economy*, Oxford: Peter Lang.

Bulgarelli, M. and M. Viviani (eds) (2006), *La promozione cooperativa*, Bologna: Il Mulino.

Cafaro, P. (2001), *La solidarietà efficiente: storia e prospettive del credito cooperativo in Italia 1883–2000*, Rome: Laterza.

Cohen, J. (1989), 'Deliberation and democratic legitimacy', in A. Hamlin and P. Pettit (eds), *The Good Polity*, Oxford: Blackwell, pp. 110–35.

Dahl, R. (1985), *A Preface to Economic Democracy*, Berkeley, CA: University of California Press.

Defourny, J and R. Spear (1995), 'Economics of cooperation', in R. Spear and H. Voetz (eds), *Success and Enterprise. The Significance of Employee Ownership and Participation*, Aldershot: Avebury, pp. 34–56.

Dow, G. (2003), *Governing the Firm. Workers' Control in Theory and Practice*, Cambridge: Cambridge University Press.

Dreze, J. (1989), *Labour Management, Contracts and Capital Markets: A General Equilibrium Approach*, Oxford: Blackwell.

Dreze, J. (1993), 'Self-management and economic theory', in P. Bardhan and J. Roemer (eds), *Market Socialism: The Current Debate,* Oxford: Oxford University Press, p. 58.

Dworkin, R. (1992), 'Liberal community', in S. Avineri and A. De Shalit (eds.), *Communitarianism and Individualism*, Oxford: Oxford University Press, pp. 234–59.

Elster, J. (1989), 'Social norms and economic theory', *Journal of Economic Perspectives*, **4**, 99–117.

European Parliament (2009), *Report on the Social Economy*, 26 January, A6-0015//2009, Referee Patrizia Toia.

Fabbri, F. (1994), *Da birrocciai a imprenditori. Una strada lunga 80 anni. Storia del Consorzio Cooperative Costruzioni. 1912–1992*, Milan: Angeli.

Falk, A. and M. Kosfeld (2004), 'Distrust. The hidden cost of control', CEPR, 4512.

Fornasari, M. and V. Zamagni (1997), *Il movimento cooperativo in Italia. Un profilo storico-economico (1854–1992)*, Florence: Vallecchi.

Frey, B. (1997), *Not Just for Money. An Economic Theory of Personal*

Motivation, Cheltenham, UK and Lyme, NH, USA: Edward Elgar Publishing.

Furobotn, E. and S. Pejovich (1970), 'Property right and the behaviour of the firm in a socialist state', *Zeitschrift für National ökonomie*, **30**, 431–54.

Gibbons, R. (1998), 'Incentives in organizations', *Journal of Economic Perspectives*, **12**, 15–132.

Gide, C. (1900), *La cooperation. Conferences de propaganda*, Paris: Larose and Fories.

Greif, A. (2006), *Institutions and the Path to the Modern Economy. Lessons from Medieval Trade*, Cambridge: Cambridge University Press.

Hansmann, H. (1996), *The Ownership of Enterprise*, Cambridge, MA: Harvard University Press.

Hart, O. and J. Moore (1996), 'The governance of exchanges: members' cooperatives versus outside ownership', *Oxford Review of Economic Policy*, **12**, 53–69.

Holyoake, G.J. (1893), *History of the Rochdale Pioneers*, 3rd edn 1900, London: Swan and Sonnenschein.

Lukes, S. (1997), 'Comparing the incomparable: trade-offs and sacrifices', in R. Chang (ed.), *Incommensurability, Incomparability and Practical Reason*, Cambridge, MA: Harvard University Press, pp. 21–45.

Marshall, A. (1889), 'Cooperation', Speech at the XXI Cooperative Congress, Ipswich, reprinted in A.C. Pigon (ed.) (1925), *Memorials of Alfred Marshall*, London: Macmillan.

Mazzoli, E. and S. Zamagni (eds) (2005), *Verso una nuova teoria della cooperazione*, Bologna: Il Mulino.

McPherson, J. (2009), *A Century of Cooperation*, Ottawa: CCA.

Menzani, T. and V. Zamagni (2010), 'Cooperative networks in the Italian economy', *Enterprise and Society*, **11**(1), 98–127.

Mill, J.S. (1852), *Principles of Political Economy* (1987 edition edited by A. Kelley, Fairfield, NJ).

Nuccio, O. (1987), *Il pensiero economico italiano: le fonti (1050–1450)*, Sassari: Gallizzi.

Okun, A. (1975), The Big Trade-off, Washington, DC: The Brookings Institution.

Pelligra, V. (2007), *I paradossi della fiducia*, Bologna: Il Mulino.

Rabbeno, U. (1889), *Le società cooperative di produzione. Contributo allo studio della questione operaia*, Milan: Dumolard.

Rajagopalan, S. (ed.) (2007), *Cooperatives in 21st Century. The Road Ahead*, Punjagutta: Icfai University Press.

Rajan, R. and L. Zingales (2003), *Saving Capitalism from Capitalists*, Chicago, UIL Chicago University Press.

Reed, D. and J.J. McMurtry (eds) (2009), *Co-operatives in a Global Economy. The Challenges of Co-operation Across Borders*, Newcastle upon Tyne: Cambridge Scholars.

Sacconi, L. (ed.) (2006), *La responsabilità sociale dell'impresa*, Rome: ABI.

Samuelson, P.A. (1957), 'Wages and interest: a modern dissection of Marxian economic models', *American Economic Review*, **67**, 884–912.

Schaffner, D.J. (2004), 'The challenges facing cooperative marketers', in C.D. Merrett and N. Walzer (eds), *Cooperatives and Local Development*, New York: M.E. Sharpe, pp. 78–94.

Schlicht, E. and C. Weizsacher (1977), 'Risk financing in labour managed economies', *Zeitschrift für die gesanite staatsswissenchraft*, **133**, 53–66.

Schumpeter, J. (1934), *The Theory of Economic Development*, Cambridge, MA: MIT Press (original edn 1912, *Theorie der Wirtschaftlichen Entwicklung*, Leipzig: Duncker and Humblot).

Schumpeter, J. (1954), *History of Economic Analysis*, London: Allen and Unwin.

Sen, A. (1966), 'Labour allocation in a cooperative enterprise', *Review of Economic Studies*, **33**, reprinted in A. Sen, 1984, *Resources, Values and Development*, Cambridge, MA: Harvard University Press, 45–59.

Sen, A. (1983), 'The profit motive', *Lloyds Bank Review*, **147**, reprinted in A. Sen, 1984, *Resources, Values and Development*, Cambridge, MA: Harvard University Press, pp. 135–60.

Sen A. (1984), *Resources, Values and Development*, Cambridge, MA: Harvard University Press.

Sen, A. (1999), *Development as Freedom*, New York: Anchor Books.

Shaffer, J. (1999), *Historical Dictionary of the Cooperative Movement*, London: The Scarecrow Press.

Stigler, G. and G. Becker (1977), 'De gustibus non est disputandum', *American Economic Review*, **67**, 76–90.

Stiglitz, J.E. (1994), *Whither Socialism*, Cambridge, MA: MIT Press.

Toniolo, G. (1900), 'Discorso di chiusura del congresso internazionale delle casse rurali e operaie', Paris, reprinted in G. Toniolo (1951),

Opera Omnia, Section IV, v. 3, Vatican City: Tipografia Poliglotta Vaticana.

Valenti, G. (1902), *L'associazione coooperativa. Contributo alla teoria economica della cooperazione,* Modena: Archivio giuridico.

Vergnanini, A. (1907), *Cooperazione integrale. Notizie sulle cooperative reggiane,* Cremona.

Virgili, F. (1924), *Cooperazione nella dottrina e nella legislazione,* 2nd edn, Milan: Hoepli.

Walras, A. (1865), *Les associations populaires de consummation de production et de credit,* Paris: Dentu.

Walzer N. and C. Merrett (eds) (2000), *A Cooperative Approach to Local Economic Development,* Westport, CT: Greenwood Publishing Group.

Ward, B. (1958), 'The firm in Illyria: market syndicalism', *American Economic Review,* **48,** 566–89.

Webb, S. and B. (1921), *The Consumers' Cooperative Movement,* London: Longman.

Williams, R.C. (2007), *The Cooperative Movement,* Aldershot: Ashgate.

Zamagni, S. (2005), 'Happiness and individualism: a very difficult union', in L. Bruni and P. Porta (eds), *Economics and Happiness,* Oxford: Oxford University Press, pp. 303–34.

Zamagni, S. (2006), 'The ethical anchoring of corporate social responsibility', in L. Zsolnai (ed.), *Interdisciplinary Yearbook of Business Ethics,* vol. I, Oxford: Peter Lang, pp. 31–51.

Zamagni, S. (2008), 'Reciprocity, civil economy, common good', in M. Archer and P. Donati (eds), *Pursuing the Common Good,* Vatican City: The Pontifical Academy of Social Sciences, pp. 467–502.

Zamagni, S., P. Sacco and P. Vanin (2006), 'The economics of human relationships', in S.C. Kolm and J. Mercier Ythier (eds), *Handbook of the Economics of Giving, Altruism and Reciprocity,* vol. I, Amsterdam: Elsevier, pp. 696–726.

Zamagni, V. (2002), *Camst: ristorazione e socialità,* Bologna: Il Mulino.

Zamagni, V. and E. Felice (2006), *Oltre il secolo. Le trasformazioni del sistema cooperativo Legacoop alla fine del secondo millennio,* Bologna: Il Mulino.

Zamagni, V., P. Battilani and A. Casali (2004), *La cooperazione di consumo in Italia,* Bologna: Il Mulino.

Zangheri, R., G. Galasso and V. Castronovo (1987), *Storia del movimento cooperativo in Italia. La Lega Nazionale delle Cooperative e Mutue (1886–1986),* Turin: Einaudi.

Zaninelli, S. (1996) (ed.), *Mezzo secolo di ricerche sulla cooperazione bianca. Risultati e prospettive*, 3 vols, Verona: Società Cattolica di Assicurazione.

Zevi, A. (2005), "Il finanziamento delle cooperative", in E. Mazzoli and S. Zamagni (eds), *Verso una nuova teoria della cooperazione*, Bologna: Il Mulino, pp. 292–330.

Zuppiroli, M. and G. Vecchio (2006), *L'utilità distintiva misurata*, Bologna: Il Mulino.

Index